Southern Italian Cooking

Dita d'Apostoli / Apostles' Fingers (page 121)

150 Healthy Regional Recipes

Southern Italian Cooking

Valentina Harris

PAVILION

The author wishes to thank Mandy Duncan Smith for her support, and for providing so many of the props; and Lucy Chamberlain for her unfailing enthusiasm and boundless energy.

First published in Great Britain in 1993 by Pavilion Books Limited
26 Upper Ground, London SE1 9PD

Text and recipes copyright
© Valentina Harris 1993
Photographs copyright
© Roger Stowell 1993
Cooking and styling of food by
Valentina Harris

The moral right of the author has been asserted

Designed by Atelier

A CIP catalogue record for this book is available from the British Library

ISBN 1 85145 843 3

Printed and bound in Italy by Graphicom

2 4 6 8 10 9 7 5 3 1

This book may be ordered by post direct from the publisher. Please contact the Marketing Department. But try your bookshop first.

Contents

Rome
and
Lazio

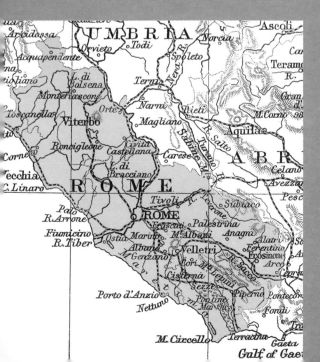

Rome and Lazio

In geographical terms, Lazio is the most varied of all the eight regions of the south. The same cannot be said for its gastronomy. Lazio's food is not for the faint-hearted, the squeamish or those seeking a light diet. They say that the people of this region have always been far too busy fighting battles, working the land and building their monuments to spend too much time fussing around in the kitchen. What comes out of these kitchens are strong flavours which make a huge impact on your taste buds, dense, heavy textures that really make you feel as though you have eaten, dishes made for huge, virile appetites.

Because the region is so heavily dominated by Rome and her glories, the region seems to be, essentially, the land which surrounds the capital. The other provinces of Viterbo, Rieti, Frosinone and Latina have to struggle hard for their own identity. But despite the dominating presence of the Eternal City, Lazio has its own individual beauty. There are mountains, lakes and rivers, rich vineyards and the huge expanse of fertile countryside called La Campagna Romana. To the north of the region most of the mountains are of volcanic origin, but as you cross the Tiber and move south, the contours become less harsh, until you reach the gentle slopes of the Colli Albani, (home of, amongst other things, the ubiquitous wine of Frascati). Once beyond this rich, luscious greenery you begin to get a sense of really having reached the South. Arid, crumbling, harsh and stony, the mountains of southern Lazio are unyielding and give you a sense of what is to come as you travel further down the boot of Italy.

The coastline stretches from the ancient Etruscan settlement of Tarquinia, in the north, to the port of Gaeta, in the south. Gaeta is famous for its excellent olives, and at Tarquinia, the frescoes on the walls of the tombs indicate that these early settlers were just as keen on eating as their successors are! At the mouth of the River Tiber is Ostia, once the port of Ancient Rome, where goods arrived from all over the Empire to fill the city's coffers and their stomachs, and now Rome's main beach, where city dwellers come for a day at the seaside. Its flat grey sand is covered with rows and rows of beach umbrellas, lined up like soldiers on parade. Further south, the tiny little islands of Ponza and Ischia are much less crowded and over developed, though also very popular. The sea breezes have an enormous influence on the climate of the entire region and provide some relief for the cities during the stifling summer heat.

The coastal areas provide a wealth of fish dishes, with everything from seafood sauces heavy with garlic, for tossing with pasta, to great bowls of *telline* (a very small flat shell fish of which you need several hundred to make a meal) or casseroles of squid with vegetables or pulses.

Inland, Lazio boasts a fantastic thermal spa at Fiuggi, from which comes one of the country's best selling mineral waters. There is stunning countryside surrounding the volcanic lakes of Bolsena, Vico, Bracciano, Albano and the tiny Nemi, also known as Diana's Mirror. Bomarzo has its famous garden full of monster statuary, and Tivoli its gardens of fountains. There is the little town of Amatrice, where they created the classic

Amatriciana sauce for pasta that has since gone on to become a world-famous dish. There are beautiful hilltop towns, notably Terni, Orvieto and Zagarolo, all of them famous for their simple trattorias serving basic country food: dishes such as roasted baby lamb smothered in herbs, oil and garlic, as well as huge, thick pasta and vegetable soups containing the best that Rome's market gardens can provide.

Like the mosaics on the floors of the ancient ruins which lie scattered all over the region as testimony to the region's illustrious history, Lazio is a mixture of very old and very new; of arid, abandoned stretches of countryside and bustling provincial towns, green pastures and narrow cobbled streets, sleepy fishing ports and roaring cargo docks.

At the centre of Lazio, in every sense, lies Rome. Here you will be able to taste the cuisine of every region in the country. Rome has excellent Piedmontese, Sardinian and Lombard restaurants, as well as Japanese eating houses and establishments where high-quality French cuisine can be enjoyed. But what of Roman food? This is slightly more difficult to obtain, but I am delighted to say that it is at last becoming easier to indulge in the real cuisine of the city.

If there is a slight apprehension on the part of the local patrons about serving the dishes of Rome to non Romans it probably has something to do with their choice of ingredients. After all, tripe (which is one of the milder offal dishes on offer here), is not to everybody's taste. Where did the idea of eating so much offal come from?

If you actually analyse the genuinely Roman specialities, you will notice that a great many of its recipes are based on ingredients which most cooks, in an ideal world, would not actually *choose* to cook. There is a historical explanation for this. Almost all these dishes sprang up in the eighteenth and nineteenth centuries around the Testaccio area of the city, where a handful of genuinely authentic Roman restaurants are still making and serving them. This is where Rome's poor lived, and also where Rome's main slaughterhouse was situated.

But the meat which came out of this sumptuously decorated building (nowadays used for trendy fashion shows and rock concerts) was destined for the tables of cardinals and dukes, and in any case the poorer inhabitants of the city, unlike their relatives who enjoyed a considerably healthier life in the country, could not afford to buy meat. The ordinary people of Rome were left to pick up the discarded scraps on the slaughterhouse floor, and thus the tradition of cooking the tail of the ox to make *Coda alla Vaccinara*, and the very strong tasting and very chewy *Insalata di Nervetti*, to mention but two, was born.

There was no sophisticated refrigeration in those days, and the heat of a Roman summer is something which cannot be overlooked – which is why strong flavourings came into general use. Spices such as cloves (as in Garofolato, see recipe page 29) and herbs such as mint and rosemary were used in conjunction with vinegar, anchovies and capers to overpower the smell and flavour of food which was often well past its sell-by date.

Fortunately, these were flavours which appealed

to the strong, lusty, warm-hearted and open nature of the Romans. The food they prepared went with their way of life, their love of gathering friends and family around a table to spend hours enjoying each other's enjoyment. Their noisy, brazen character and their passionate love of life, coupled with their in-bred, unshakeable pride in being part of the great city – all this has found a gastronomic expression in feasts of *abbacchio, coratella* and potato *gnocchi* with pork sausages in rich tomato sauces.

Put the offal and meat dishes of Rome alongside the plethora of vegetables which come from the rich countryside; add the lamb dishes and the ewe's milk cheeses like Pecorino and Ricotta that are born of the culinary traditions of the shepherds of Lazio (the *Zampognari,* who have always had links with next door Abruzzi); scatter in the fish specialities of the coastal towns; add a few local recipe pastries and cakes (the two most famous are the oval, whipped cream-filled *Maritozzi* and the deep fried *Bigné di San Giuseppe*); douse the whole thing with rivers of the white wines of Frascati, or the intriguingly named Est! Est! Est!, or the ancient, strong, heady red called Falerno . . . and you will have understood the cuisine of Lazio.

Later on, over a leisurely espresso which you will sip very slowly, perhaps in the shadow of some ancient monument, you can indulge yourself in the digestive qualities of a tiny glass of Sambuca, and reflect that this too is a local product. To be exact, it originated in the town of Viterbo.

Once you have got to grips with the strong, fiery assault on your digestive system which is about to occur as you travel further south, it is best to abandon any notion you might have of enjoying much in the way of delicately flavoured little morsels. For this is food which appeals to the eye and perfumes the air, food which has a whole range of different textures and where the flavour is always uncompromising, always direct. Lazio is a good place to start our culinary journey, as it prepares you fairly gently for the assault which the cooking of southern Italy is going to make on your senses.

Supplì alla Romana / Roman Rice Fritters (page 12)

Panzerotti alla Romana

Roman Cheese and Ham Fritters

Probably one of the most traditional recipes from the culinary history of this great city. I can remember eating those wrapped in paper, walking along the street from the bus stop, or having huge batches of them frying at home of an afternoon when the garden was strewn with young guests. We were always hungry in those days, and in-between-meal-snacks never seemed to make any difference to our waistlines!

This recipe is the same age as I am, and seems to have fallen into disuse these days, although I am reviving it by making *panzerotti* for my sons! Serve as an antipasto or as an afternoon snack.

Makes about 8 to 10

125g/4oz/1 cup Gruyère cheese, finely
    cubed
75g/3oz prosciutto crudo (Parma ham),
    chopped
1 heaped tablespoon grated Parmesan
    cheese
1 egg, beaten
salt and freshly milled black pepper
350g/12oz/3 cups plain (all-purpose)
    flour
50g/2oz/¼ cup unsalted butter, cubed
2 egg yolks
2–3 tablespoons cold water
1 egg white, lightly beaten until frothy
vegetable oil for deep-frying

Mix the cubed cheese with the prosciutto, Parmesan and the whole egg. Season with a little salt and pepper.

Pile all the flour on the worktop and make a hollow in the centre with your fist. Put a pinch of flour, the butter and the egg yolks into the hollow. Blend together with your fingertips, adding a little cold water, if necessary.

When you have achieved a smooth ball of dough, roll it out as thinly as possible and cut it into circles with a pastry cutter or up-turned tumbler. Put a spoonful of the cheese mixture on each circle and fold the circles in half, brushing the edges with a little beaten egg white. Seal the *panzerotti* closed.

Put the oil for deep-frying into a deep-fat fryer and heat until a small square of bread tossed into the oil sizzles instantly. Fry the *panzerotti* in batches, if necessary, until golden brown and puffy, about 5 minutes each. Drain very thoroughly on kitchen paper (paper towels). Serve at once, piping hot.

Supplì alla Romana

Roman Rice Fritters

Supplì seem to be as popular now as they ever were everywhere in Rome. A friend recently returned from a visit to Rome and described an amazing delicacy which he had sampled. He described them in such glowing terms that I had a little trouble in understanding just what it was he had eaten, and he could not remember what they were called. Once I had asked him where he had eaten them, it all became clear: he had fallen victim to the fantastic flavour and texture of the wonderful *supplì* that are served at the famous Roman café and catering company called simply Euclide. I really recommend you try one, if you ever happen to be in my beloved Roma, but in the meanwhile, make your own! Serve as an antipasto or an afternoon snack.

Serves 4

25g/1oz/½ cup dried porcini mushrooms
4 canned tomatoes, well drained, seeded
    and coarsely chopped
125g/4oz/½ cup butter, cubed
300g/19oz risotto rice
salt and freshly milled black pepper
2 eggs, beaten
2 heaped tablespoons freshly grated
    Parmesan cheese
½ tablespoon lard
½ small onion, peeled and finely chopped
2 chicken livers, trimmed and finely
    chopped
50g/2oz prosciutto crudo (Parma ham),
    chopped
90g/3½oz minced (ground) veal or beef
1 tablespoon tomato purée (paste), diluted
    in 4 tablespoons warm water
125g/4oz/1 cup mozzarella cheese, finely
    cubed
3 tablespoons plain white (all-purpose)
    flour
1 egg, beaten
3 tablespoons fine breadcrumbs
vegetable oil for deep frying

Cover the dried mushrooms in warm water and
leave to stand for about 15 mins.

Pour the cold water into a saucepan, add the
tomatoes and 75g/3oz/6 tablespoons of the
butter and bring to the boil. As soon as it boils,
add the rice and stir thoroughly. Season with a
little salt and cook until just tender, about
12 minutes, being careful not to let it overcook.
Take it off the heat and stir in the eggs and the

Parmesan. Tip the rice out on to the worktop
and spread it out. Leave to cool.

Meanwhile, put the remaining butter into
another saucepan with the lard. Add the onion and
fry for about 5 minutes. Add the chicken livers,
prosciutto and minced (ground) meat. Stir
together, frying gently, for about 8 minutes. Add
the diluted tomato purée (paste) and stir
thoroughly. Season with salt and pepper.

Scoop up spoonfuls of cooked rice and shape
into balls about the size of an egg. Hold the ball
and make a deep hole in the rice with the index
finger on your other hand. Insert some tomato
sauce and a few cubes of cheese into each rice ball,
making sure you squeeze closed the hole afterwards
with rice. Repeat until all the rice is used.

Roll the rice balls in flour, then the egg and
finally the breadcrumbs. Heat the oil in a deep-fat
fryer until a small piece of bread dropped into the
oil sizzles instantly.

Fry the rice balls in batches, if necessary, until
golden brown and crisp, for about 3 minutes each,
then scoop them out of the oil with a slotted
spoon and drain thoroughly on kitchen paper
(paper towels). Serve piping hot.

Frittata di Zucchine
Flat Courgette Omelette

These flat omelettes (omelets) are typical of Italian
cooking all over the country. In Rome and the
surrounding area, they are often served cold as part
of the antipasto course, sometimes accompanied by
a dish of pickles for extra piquancy.

Serves 6

4–5 courgettes (zucchini), topped and
    tailed and sliced
1 tablespoon lard or dripping, or
    2 tablespoons olive oil
½ large onion, thinly sliced
2 tablespoons chopped fresh parsley
6 eggs, thoroughly beaten
salt and freshly milled black pepper

Place the courgettes (zucchini) into a large frying
pan (skillet), preferably non-stick, with the lard,
dripping or oil. Add the onion and the parsley and
fry the courgettes gently until just soft.

When the courgettes are cooked, spread them
around the pan in a relatively even layer and pour
over the eggs. Wait for the eggs to set and then
cover the pan with a large lid or heatproof platter.
Turn the omelette (omelet) over on to the lid or
platter, then slide it back into the pan the other
way up. Cook it on the other side for about 5
minutes, then slide on to a serving dish. You can
eat it at once or leave it to cool and serve it cold.

Spiedini di Provatura

Grilled Cheese with Anchovies

Provatura is basically a Roman version of
mozzarella cheese. It is traditionally made with
buffalo milk and is about the size and shape of a
large egg. It tends to be slightly more solid and less
creamy and soft than mozzarella. If you cannot get
hold of provatura, you can use scamorza, which is
matured and sometimes smoked mozzarella, or

fresh mozzarella which has been allowed to harden
slightly over three or four days. Really fresh, white
and whey-filled mozzarella is perfect for salads and
to be eaten on its own. Once more than two days
old, however, it is better to cook it. This is a very
useful recipe for using up mozzarella which is past
its best. It is delicious cooked over a barbecue and
excellent made using a grill (broiler).

Makes about 8

350g/12oz provatura, scamorza or
    mozzarella cheese
a small loaf of coarse, crusty bread, or
    sliced white bread
150g/5oz/⅔ cup unsalted butter
2 large salted anchovies, boned, rinsed and
    patted dry
2 tablespoons milk
freshly milled black pepper

Cut the cheese and the bread into equal-sized
circles about 2cm/¾in thick each. Thread them
alternately on to wooden skewers, making sure they
are packed as tightly as possible.

Grill (broil) or barbecue until the cheese is just
running and the bread is crisp and toasted.

Meanwhile, put the butter and the anchovies
into a little saucepan and warm over a low heat,
stirring constantly until the anchovies reduce to
a smooth cream. Add the milk as the mixture
begins to amalgamate. Season with freshly milled
black pepper.

Arrange the grilled cheese on a serving platter,
cover with the anchovy sauce and serve at once.

Frittata di Zucchine/Flat Courgette Omelette (page 13)

Minestra alla Viterbese

Vegetable Soup with Semolina

This is a typical country summertime soup, prepared when all the vegetables are at their peak of lusciousness, swollen with ripeness. I like to eat this on summer evenings when there is a hint of coolness in the evening air, and I can sit outside and enjoy the sweet scents of the garden plants while the swallows wheel and shriek overhead. The pretty town of Viterbo has quite a few specialities, and the recipes, like this one, seem to have lasted the test of time remarkably well.

Serves 4 to 6

1 large clove garlic
1 large stick celery
8 sprigs fresh parsley
9 leaves fresh basil
1 large potato, peeled
1 large carrot, scraped
1 large, very ripe tomato, peeled and
   chopped
1 large courgette (zucchini), topped and
   tailed and cut into thin matchsticks
1 large onion, peeled and thinly sliced
50g/2oz/¾ cup semolina
25g/1oz/2 tablespoons unsalted butter,
   diced
50g/2oz/½ cup freshly grated Parmesan
   cheese

Chop the garlic, celery, parsley and basil very finely. Grate the potato and the carrot and mix together.

Tip all the vegetables into a saucepan. Add 1.2 litres/2 pints (5 cups) cold water and slowly bring to the boil. Simmer for 15 minutes, covered.

Trickle the semolina into the simmering soup in a very fine 'rain', stirring constantly. Simmer for a further 15 minutes, stirring occasionally.

Remove from the heat, stir in the butter and the cheese and leave to cool slightly before serving.

Minestra di Riso e Fave

Rice and Broad Bean Soup

From springtime onwards, broad (fava) beans are sold at roadside kiosks which sporadically line the route from the airport into the heart of Rome. One of the most perfect flavour combinations in the world has got to be fresh, tender broad beans coupled with soft and crumbly, incredibly strong tasting pecorino cheese. Both reach their peak at the same time, when the ewes have plenty of milk for the spring lambs, and extra for cheese making!

Serves 4

50g/2oz/¼ cup lard
1 large onion, peeled and finely chopped
1kg/2lb fresh broad (fava) beans (weight
   with pods), shelled
8 tablespoons hot water
2 tablespoons tomato purée (paste)
200g/7oz/1 cup short-grain rice
25g/1oz/2 tablespoons unsalted butter
salt and freshly milled black pepper
125g/4oz/1 cup Pecorino cheese, freshly
   grated

Chop the lard and the onion together to make a kind of blended mass, called *battuto* in Italian. Fry this slowly until the onion is soft. Add the broad (fava) beans to the sizzling hot onion and lard. Stir the hot water and tomato purée (paste), then add this to the broad beans. Season with salt and freshly milled black pepper.

Stir well, then simmer for about 10 minutes. Stir in the rice, then add the butter and stir again.

Heat 1.12 litres/2 pints/5 cups water until just boiling, then season with salt. Gradually stir this into the rice and broad bean mixture, stirring constantly and keeping a slow rolling boil going. Serve as soon as the rice is tender, with plenty of freshly grated pecorino cheese for sprinkling over the top.

Brodetto Romano

Roman Broth

Traditionally, this was the soup which would appear on the table of every household as the opening course for the Easter feast. Sadly, it is falling into disuse, as much more sophisticated and up-market (up-scale) ingredients take precedence over the more old-fashioned dishes, linked inexorably to the custom and ritual. It is the breast of lamb which gives this soup its particular flavour.

Allow two days for the preparation of this dish. The success of this soup depends almost entirely on the quality of the stock used. Put your efforts into this with love and care and you will not be disappointed by the results.

Serves 6

750g/1½lb lamb breast
750g/1½lb chicken pieces
300g/10oz marrow bone
300g/10oz veal shin
2 sticks celery
2 carrots, scraped
2 small tomatoes
1 large onion, peeled
1 bay leaf
small bunch fresh mixed herbs, tied
    together with string or a ready made
    bouquet garni
salt
3 black peppercorns
6 egg yolks
juice of ½ lemon
8 slices ciabatta bread, toasted and cubed
1 teaspoon fresh marjoram leaves, finely
    chopped
6 heaped tablespoons freshly grated
    Parmesan cheese
6 teaspoons chopped fresh parsley

Pour 1.8 litres/3 pints/7½ cups cold water into a large stockpot and add all the raw meat and the celery, carrot, tomatoes, onion and all the herbs. Season with salt and add the peppercorns. Cover and slowly bring to the boil, forcing the flavours from all these ingredients to seep into the water, thus transforming it into a sublime *brodo*. Leave the stock to simmer, covered, for about 3 hours, skimming the surface occasionally.

Remove it from the heat, leave it to stand and cool completely. Strain it carefully and leave it to stand again. Refrigerate overnight.

The following day, remove the surface layer of fat. Strain again, and measure — you will need a generous 1.5 litres/2½ pints/6 cups to serve 6 people. Return to the heat and bring to the boil, tightly covered, then take off the heat.

Meanwhile, beat the egg yolks thoroughly in a second saucepan with the lemon juice. Gradually whisk in the hot stock. Return to a very low heat and continue to whisk over a very low heat. Do **not** allow this mixture to boil. It must not go stringy like *stracciatella*, which is a completely different soup altogether. Just heat it through very gently, whisking all the time.

Divide the bread cubes evenly between 6 soup plates, sprinkle evenly with the marjoram, Parmesan and parsley. Pour over the very hot soup to fill each plate. Serve at once.

Pasta e Broccoli con Brodo di Arzilla

Broccoli and Pasta Soup with Sting Ray Broth

I use the name sting ray for this fish with some trepidation, because I have been unable to find out what the official name for this fish might be. I call it sting ray because that is what it looks like, and because I suspect that the flavour of a sting ray is not unlike that of this very cheap and unloved fish! In Italian it is called *arzilla* and is symbolic of the era in Rome's culinary history when people were starving and forced to survive on the scraps which the gentry refused to partake of. They say that at the fish markets, or on the docksides, the *arzilla* would have been thrown aside during the selection of more palatable fish for the Vatican or the royal court. I would like to think that the ugly, almost meatless arzilla was pounced upon with eager hands and that this quite wonderful soup was then created out of it. It makes excellent, strong-flavoured stock, which is the basis of the soup.

Serves 4

1kg/2lb sting ray, very fresh and very
   carefully cleaned
1 clove garlic, peeled
1 onion, peeled and halved
1 stick celery
salt and freshly milled black pepper
4 tablespoons olive oil
1 clove garlic, finely chopped
½ dried red chilli pepper, finely chopped
1 anchovy fillet preserved in oil, drained
   and rinsed
250g/8oz/scant 1 cup canned tomatoes,
   drained and coarsely chopped
½ wine glass dry white wine
1 green Romanesco cauliflower
200g/7oz/1 cup small pasta tubes, such as
   avemarie or cannolicchi

Place the fish in a saucepan. Cover with 1.2 litres/2 pints/5 cups water and add the whole clove of garlic, the halved onion and the celery stick whole. Season with salt and pepper and bring to a gentle boil. Reduce to a simmer, then cover and cook slowly for 10–15 minutes.

Remove the fish from the water. Cut off the 'fringes', the head, the tail and all the cartilages. Put the flesh from the fish aside and return all the rest, including the skin, to the saucepan. Simmer for a further 30 minutes. Remove from the heat, strain and leave to cool.

Dried Porcini Soaking

In a separate saucepan, heat the olive oil gently and fry the garlic and chilli for about 5 minutes. Add the anchovy fillet, stir and fry for a further 5 minutes. Add the tomatoes to the fried garlic mixture, then stir in the wine and boil off the alcohol for 1 minute. Reduce the heat to a slow simmer. Add 5–6 tablespoons of the fish stock, cover and simmer for about 20 minutes.

Break the cauliflower into small florets (flowerets), peeling the stalks (stems) of the woodier pieces. Add these to the tomato and garlic mixture and stir together very thoroughly. Add the remaining stock and return to the boil.

After about 8 minutes, add the pasta and continue to simmer until it is tender. Flake the flesh from the fish and stir it into the soup. Transfer the soup to a tureen and serve immediately.

Pancotto con l'Olio

Bread Soup

This very simple soup appears in various guises all over Italy. Reflecting the nature of the cuisine of Lazio, which is by its very nature filled with the strong tastes of garlic, anchovies and herbs, however, it seems only natural that the version from Rome should have a much stronger flavour and an altogether gutsier appearance and taste than any of the other very similar soups from other regions.

Serves 4

2 large cloves garlic, crushed
75ml/3fl oz/5 tablespoons olive oil
350g/12oz fresh ripe tomatoes, peeled, seeded and coarsely chopped
salt and freshly milled black pepper
200g/7oz stale bread, broken into hazelnut-sized pieces
½ teaspoon dried marjoram
4 tablespoons freshly grated pecorino cheese
extra olive oil, to serve

Pour 1.8 litres/3 pints/7½ cups water into a saucepan with the garlic and half the oil. Add the tomatoes and season with salt. Bring to the boil slowly.

Add the bread and simmer, stirring occasionally, for about 20 minutes.

Remove from the heat and stir in the remaining oil. Add the marjoram, the cheese and plenty of freshly milled black pepper. Stir and transfer to a tureen. Serve at once with more olive oil for each person to add to their own serving, if they wish.

Uova al Tegamino con Pomodoro

Baked Eggs with Tomatoes

A delightfully simple dish to serve with plenty of crusty bread and a green salad.

Serves 4

500g/1lb/2 cups canned tomatoes,
    drained, seeded and chopped
salt and freshly milled black pepper
3 tablespoons olive oil
8 fresh eggs

Pre-heat the oven to 220°C/425°F/Gas Mark 7.
    Put the tomatoes into a saucepan with about 2 tablespoons water and 2 pinches of salt. Cover and simmer very slowly for about 30 minutes, stirring occasionally.
    Remove the pan from the heat and push the tomato sauce through a sieve (strainer). Pour the oil into an ovenproof dish and then pour the sauce on top of the oil. Break the eggs into the dish on top of the sauce and sprinkle with pepper. Bake for about 5 minutes, or until the eggs are just set but the yolks are still runny. Serve at once.

Nociata

Pasta with Walnut Sauce

This is one of those rather strange old recipes which obviously had a completely logical place on the table at the time when it was concocted. Nowadays, the traditional nature of Christmas has been more than a little warped. It is a recipe which was created to be a part of the Christmas Eve feast, when this very special meal had a much more ritualistic atmosphere about it than royal turkey and trimmings! If you like sweet-but-savoury flavours, then this is a perfect dish for you. Serve this hot or cold.

Serves 4

salt
250g/12oz short, stubby pasta shapes,
    such as penne, conchiglie or maccheroni
150g/5oz/1 cup shelled walnuts, broken
50g/2oz/¼ cup sugar
grated rind (peel) of 1 large lemon
1 teaspoon ground cinnamon
25g/1oz/2 tablespoons unsalted butter

Bring a large saucepan of salted water to a rolling boil. Toss in the pasta, return to the boil and cook until just tender; check the packet for exact cooking time as brands vary. Make sure the pasta is not overcooked.

Meanwhile, put the walnuts into a food processor using the blade attachment and process to a fine mass with the sugar, the lemon rind (peel) and the cinnamon. Alternatively, pound the walnuts with a pestle and mortar and mix in the sugar, lemon rind and cinnamon.

Transfer the walnut mixture into the dish from which you intend to serve the pasta. Drain the pasta carefully and put it into the serving dish on top of the walnut mixture. Add the butter. Mix everything together to distribute the walnut sauce evenly, then leave to stand for about 5 minutes covered, before serving.

Pasta e Patate

Pasta with Potatoes

This is the kind of hearty, filling, very thick soup which epitomizes the simplicity of peasant food. Although this is a useful winter warmer, it is also delicious served at room temperature and sprinkled with a little olive oil and chopped fresh herbs as a cool (not chilled) summer soup.

Serves 6

1 heaped tablespoon lard or dripping
1 thick slice guanciale, pancetta or smoked
   streaky bacon
1 small onion, peeled and sliced
4–5 fresh parsley sprigs
1.5 litres/2½ pints/6 cups good-quality
   meat or chicken stock
5 potatoes, peeled and cubed
300g/10oz cannolicchi, ave marie or
   similar short, stubby pasta
4 tablespoons freshly grated pecorino
   cheese

Chop together the lard or dripping, bacon, onion and parsley. Fry in a saucepan slowly over a low heat, without letting anything brown. Pour in the stock, stir and bring to the boil. Add the potatoes, cover and simmer until the potatoes are soft and almost falling apart.

Toss in the pasta, stir, return to the boil and cook until the pasta is tender. Remove from the heat, stir in the cheese and serve at once.

Risotto con le Seppie

Squid Risotto

This is not the black and inky risotto of Venice, but the strong and garlicky version of the Lazio coastline. The sweet-tasting, bland squid is a perfect backdrop for the intense flavours which typify the cuisine of the region and crop up often in various recipes.

Pasta e Ceci/Pasta with Chick-peas (page 25)

Serves 4

500g/1lb squid, cleaned and sliced into
   rings, with the tentacles cut into
   manageable sections
50ml/2fl oz/¼ cup olive oil
4 cloves garlic, crushed
1 salted anchovy, boned, rinsed and patted
   dry
3 tablespoons tomato purée (paste)
3 tablespoons chopped fresh parsley
350g/12oz/1¾ cups risotto rice
salt
½ dried red chilli pepper, crushed

Rinse and pat dry the squid. Fry the olive oil, garlic
and anchovy together in a large saucepan until the
garlic is just soft, stirring frequently. Add the
tomato purée (paste) and the squid. Stir everything
together, simmer for about 5 minutes and then add
enough cold water to cover generously. Do not add
salt at this stage because it will make the squid
become very rubbery.

   Cover and simmer very slowly for about 2
hours, adding more water if necessary. When the
squid is completely tender, add the chopped parsley
and the rice. Stir together and continue to cook,
adding boiling water occasionally and stirring
continuously. Only add water when the rice has
absorbed all the liquid and is dried out. As soon as
the rice is tender, stir in salt and crushed chilli
pepper to taste. Stir together and transfer to a
platter to serve.

Ravioli con la Ricotta
Ravioli with Ricotta Stuffing

Prepared most frequently from October to
February, when there is plenty of ewe's milk
available for the preparation of the ewe's milk
ricotta which gives it the special flavour, this is a
delicious dish. Ordinary cow's milk ricotta,
however, works perfectly adequately.

   It is very important to make the filling first,
and to let it stand until required. Some people
make a sweet version, add nutmeg, sugar or
cinnamon to the filling. If you do so, omit the
Parmesan and the salt and pepper.

Serves 4

350g/12oz/1½ cups fresh ricotta cheese
3 eggs, beaten
salt and freshly milled black pepper
3 heaped tablespoon freshly grated
   Parmesan cheese
400g/14oz/heaped 3 cups plain (all-
   purpose) flour
4 eggs
125g/4oz/½ cup unsalted butter, melted
extra 50g/2oz/½ cup freshly grated
   Parmesan cheese, to serve

First make the filling. Push the ricotta through a
fine sieve (strainer) twice. Beat the eggs, a little salt
and pepper and the Parmesan. Gradually add the
ricotta, beating constantly. Set aside until required.

Pile all the flour on the worktop and make a hollow in the centre with your fist. Break the eggs into the centre and add a pinch of salt. Blend the eggs into the flour using your fingertips, then use your entire hand to knead into a smooth dough. Knead until elastic and smooth, then roll out several times until really elastic and slightly shiny. Cut into 2 equal-sized sheets.

Arrange rows of the ricotta filling equal distance apart on 1 sheet, leaving a finger-wide gap around each mound of filling. Cover with the second sheet of pasta dough, then run a pastry wheel between and across each row to cut out even-sized, square ravioli. Leave them to dry on the worktop for about 5 minutes.

Bring a large saucepan of salted water to a rolling boil. Slide in the ravioli, return to the boil and cook until just tender, about 6 minutes. Remove them from the boiling water with a fish slice (pancake turner) and arrange on a flat platter in layers, covering each layer with melted butter and a sprinkling of extra Parmesan. Serve at once.

Pasta e Ceci

Pasta with Chick-peas

According to some experts, this is the oldest known recipe for pasta. Apparently, the ancient Romans often served this dish in a format known as *laganum et ciceris*, which consisted of boiled chick-peas mixed with thin strips of a pancake (crêpe) made out of fried gruel. The dish was finally finished off with a generous dressing of fermented fish sauce. I think you will agree that the following recipe is considerably more palatable!

Like so many recipes from this region, this is excellent either piping hot in winter, or cool (but not chilled) in the summer.

Serves 6

300g/10oz/1¾ cups dried chick-peas
9 cloves garlic, chopped to a purée
9 tablespoons olive oil
2 5cm/2in sprigs fresh rosemary
salt and freshly milled black pepper
6 salted anchovy fillets, rinsed, dried and
    very finely chopped
2 tablespoons tomato purée (paste)
300g/10oz cannolicchi, ave marie or
    similar short, small stubby pasta
To garnish:
1–3 tablespoons olive oil
4 twists of the pepper-mill

Put the chick-peas into a large bowl and cover generously with cold water. Leave to soak overnight. Drain and rinse the beans thoroughly. Place in a saucepan and cover with plenty of cold water, bring to the boil and boil for about 5 minutes, then drain and rinse again. Set aside for the moment.

In a large, deep saucepan, fry together half the garlic and 3 tablespoons of the oil for about 5 minutes. Add the chick-peas and stir together thoroughly. Pour in about 1.5 litres/2½ pints/6 cups cold water and add the rosemary. Stir, season with pepper, cover and simmer for about 1 hour or until the chick-peas are soft and slightly mushy. Season with salt.

Meanwhile, fry the remaining garlic and oil in a separate small pan with the anchovy fillets and the tomato purée (paste) stirring frequently. When the mixture is cooked through and perfectly amalgamated, remove from the heat but keep warm. When the chick-peas are cooked, add the pasta to the soup. Check that there is still sufficient liquid to cook it properly, adding a little water, if necessary. Stir, return to the boil and cook the pasta until just tender, then stir in the anchovy and garlic mixture. Remove from the heat. Transfer the soup into 6 bowls and coat the surface of each one with a little drizzle of oil and a small sprinkling of fresh black pepper.

Fettuccine alla Romana

Roman Fettuccine

Fettuccine are the Roman version of what are called tagliatelle in Emilia Romagna, thin ribbons of delicious fresh pasta which require only a couple of minutes in boiling salted water to cook, and are then dressed with a variety of sauces. You can, of course, buy ready made fresh pasta if you prefer, or use dried fettuccine or tagliatelle instead.

In this recipe, the sauce is a rich and meaty tomato sauce which needs the addition of a couple of tablespoons of the sauce from Garofolata (page 29) to give it a mild flavour of cloves for genuine authenticity.

Serves 4

for the pasta:
400g/14oz/heaped 3 cups plain white (all-purpose) flour
4 eggs
salt
extra flour for worktop

for the sauce:
50g/2oz/¼ cup fat from prosciutto crudo (Parma ham), finely chopped
1 large clove garlic, finely chopped
1 small onion, peeled and finely chopped
350g/12oz/1½ cups canned tomatoes, seeded and coarsely chopped
15g/½oz dried mushrooms, soaked in hand hot water to cover for 20 minutes, then drained
25g/1oz/2 tablespoons unsalted butter
250g/8oz chicken livers, trimmed and chopped
4 tablespoons dry white wine
4 tablespoons chicken stock, hot
3 tablespoons sauce from Garofolato (page 29), optional
salt and freshly milled black pepper
25g/1oz/2 tablespoons unsalted butter
6 tablespoons freshly grated Parmesan or pecorino cheese, or a mixture of the 2, to serve

Salsicce con Broccoletti/Sausages with Sprouting Broccoli (page 32)

First make the pasta. Pile all the flour on the worktop and make a hollow in the centre with your fist, then break the eggs into the hollow. Mix the eggs into the flour with your fingertips, gradually mixing in more and more of the flour until you are obliged to use your whole hand. Knead very thoroughly, until you have a smooth and very elastic dough. Roll it out several times, folding it over and rolling it again each time. Finally, roll it out as finely as possible and cut it into 1cm/½ inch strips. Scatter the noodles on a floured surface and leave them to rest under a cloth until required.

Now move on to the sauce. Fry the fat and the garlic together until the fat has run and the garlic is golden brown. Be very careful not to let the fat or the garlic burn, keeping the heat low. Add the onion and continue to fry until transparent. Stir in the tomatoes and mushrooms, then leave to simmer, covered for 20 minutes.

In a separate pan, melt the butter and fry the chicken livers gently until browned all over, about 3 minutes. Sprinkle over the wine and allow the alcohol to burn off for about 1 minute, then stir in the stock. Cover and simmer very, very slowly for about 10 minutes. Tip the chicken liver sauce into the tomato sauce. Season to taste with salt and pepper. Cover and leave to simmer gently for a further 30 minutes. Add the Garofolato sauce, if using, and heat through.

Meanwhile, bring a large pan of salted water to the boil. Toss in the pasta, return to the boil and cook, until just tender, 2–3 minutes. Drain and return to the pan. Add butter and toss together thoroughly, then pour over the sauce and toss again. Transfer on to a warmed serving dish, sprinkle with the cheese and serve at once.

Coda alla Vaccinara

Braised Oxtail

---

1 oxtail and 1 ox cheek, weighing 2kg/4lb altogether, well rinsed and cut into large chunks
125g/4oz pork belly (belly of pork) or bacon (slab bacon), finely chopped
1 carrot, very finely chopped
1 large stick celery, very finely chopped
1 onion, peeled and very finely chopped
2 cloves garlic, very finely chopped
salt and crushed dried red chilli pepper
150ml/5fl oz dry white wine
3 tablespoons tomato purée (paste) diluted in 500ml/16fl oz/2 cups hand hot water
5 sticks celery, diced

Bring a large pan of water to the boil, then add in the chunks of meat. As soon as the water returns to the boil, remove the chunks of meat with a slotted spoon and set aside to cool.

Put the pork belly (belly of pork) into a separate saucepan with the carrot, celery, onion and garlic. Fry together gently for about 10 minutes, stirring frequently. Add the meat and brown it thoroughly all over. Season with salt and a generous pinch of crushed dried red chilli.

Add about half the wine and boil off the alcohol for about 1 minute. Pour in the diluted tomato purée (paste) and stir. Cover and leave to simmer for about 1 hour, then add the remaining wine. Boil off the alcohol, cover and simmer for a further 3 hours.

Stir in the celery and cook slowly for a further 30 minutes, until the meat is very tender. Transfer to a warm platter and serve at once.

Garofolato

Beef Stew with Cloves

This is a very old and traditional recipe from the poorer quarters of Rome, in which the use of many strongly flavoured ingredients, such as garlic and cloves, were used to cover up bad smells in the meat itself. Towards the end of the last century, the poor population of Rome could only afford to buy meat which was discarded by wealthier citizens, and it was often past its 'sell by' date once it had made its way to the kitchen.

The recipe is still in use today – even though meat is a great deal fresher! It takes its name from the clove, which in Italian is called *chiodo di garofano*, and in Roman dialect is called simply *garofalo*. The dish is used very widely, not only because it is so delicious, but also because it is very economical as all the sauce that it is made with can be used to dress pasta dishes, or added as a flavouring to casseroles, soups, stews and sauces.

Serves 4 to 6

1kg/2lb joint of beef suitable for pot
   roasting, such as topside
2 thick slices very fatty prosciutto crudo
   (Parma ham), very finely chopped
1 teaspoon dried marjoram
4 cloves garlic, crushed
salt and freshly milled black pepper
5 cloves
3 tablespoons olive oil
1 large onion, peeled and finely chopped
1 large carrot, finely chopped
1 stick celery, finely chopped
2 cloves garlic, finely chopped
1 large glass dry red wine
3 tablespoons tomato purée (paste) diluted
   with 750ml/1¼ pints/3 cups water

Wipe and trim the meat as required. Make various deep holes all over the joint with a thin sharp knife or a skewer. Mix together the chopped ham fat with the marjoram and crushed garlic. Season this mixture with plenty of salt and pepper, then insert some of this paste into each of the holes. Insert the cloves at random into the meat as well.

Heat the olive oil and fry the onion, carrot, celery and chopped garlic in a large flameproof casserole until soft, about 3 minutes. Add the meat and raise the heat to brown it all over. Lower the heat and add the wine. Let the alcohol boil off for 2 minutes, then pour on the diluted tomato purée (paste). Depending upon the size of the casserole, this should completely and abundantly cover the joint, but add more water if necessary.

Cover and simmer very slowly for about 3 hours, until the meat is completely tender. Remove the meat from the sauce and slice it on to a warmed serving platter. Serve with some of the sauce, the rest of which can be saved to be used in other dishes (see Tripe Stew, page 33) or as a dressing for plain pasta.

Baccalà in Guazzetto

Stewed Salt Cod

Eaten with almost ritualistic solemnity in the Monti quarter of Old Rome, this is a very old, almost ancient recipe. Always soak salt cod very thoroughly for about a day in several changes of water before using. When it is soft and flaky, trim it carefully and cut it into 50g/2oz chunks. Rinse and dry it thoroughly, and then use as fresh cod.

Serves 4

500g/1lb fresh ripe tomatoes
1kg/2lb salt cod
7 tablespoons olive oil
salt and freshly milled black pepper
garlic, fresh basil and fresh parsley,
    chopped together (75g/3oz altogether)

Pre-heat the oven to 190°C/375°F/Gas Mark 5. Rinse the tomatoes and place them, whole and unpeeled, in a large bowl. Bring enough water to completely submerge the tomatoes to the boil. Pour the boiling water over the tomatoes and leave to stand for 2 minutes. Remove the tomatoes and peel them, then cut into strips and discard the seeds.

Prepare the cod with care, making sure you remove all bones, then place it in a saucepan. Add enough water to just cover, then bring to the boil. Simmer for 2–3 minutes, then remove the cod with a slotted spoon. Discard the water.

Oil an ovenproof dish with about half the olive oil. Arrange the fish in a single layer. Scatter the strips of tomato over the fish. Sprinkle with salt and pepper, then add the chopped garlic and herbs. Pour over the remaining oil and bake for 30–35 minutes, until the cod is cooked through and flakes easily when tested with the tip of a knife. Serve at once.

Seppie Affogate

Stewed Squid

Use squid or octopus, depending upon what is available, to make this very simple and delicious recipe. Traditionally, very small, young and tender fish are used, but larger fish can simply be cut to size as required. If you use large octopus, it will need to be thoroughly tenderized first.

Serves 4

750g/1½lb squid or octopus, cleaned and
    trimmed; leave whole if no longer than
    6cm/2½in or cut accordingly
4 tablespoons olive oil
1 tablespoon white wine vinegar
salt and freshly milled black pepper
juice of 1 lemon
1 tablespoon chopped fresh parsley, to
    garnish

Put the squid into a wide frying pan (skillet) with the oil and vinegar. Place over a medium heat and leave until liquid from the fish seeps out, and then all the liquid evaporates completely, stirring occasionally. This takes anything from 5 to 15 minutes, or longer.

When the fish is coated in olive oil, season with salt and pepper and stir again. Leave to simmer for a further 5 minutes, then add the lemon juice. Remove from the heat, transfer to a warm dish and sprinkle with parsley. Serve at once.

Carciofi alla Romana/Artichokes with Mint (page 36)

Salsicce con Broccoletti

Sausages with Sprouting Broccoli

Strong tasting and extremely robust, this dish is typical of traditional Roman cuisine.

Serves 4

1 tablespoon lard
2 cloves garlic, crushed
1 dried red chilli pepper
500g/1lb Italian sausages
750g/1½lb sprouting broccoli, rinsed and trimmed
salt

Melt the lard and fry the garlic and chilli pepper for about 5 minutes. Add the sausages and turn them to brown all over, then cook gently for about 5 minutes. Add the broccoli. Season with a little salt and stir thoroughly.

Cover and simmer for about 20 minutes, stirring frequently and adding a little water if it appears to be drying out. Serve at once.

Rognone in Umido

Stewed Kidneys

Offal (variety meat) is a very important aspect of Roman cuisine. It crops up in many recipes, such as this one for a casserole of calves' kidneys.

Serves 4

500g/1lb calves' kidney, trimmed and very thinly sliced
1 tablespoon lard
1 large onion, peeled and finely sliced
500g/1lb fresh ripe tomatoes, peeled and seeded
3 tablespoons dry red wine
salt and freshly milled black pepper
2 tablespoons chopped fresh parsley

Put the sliced kidneys into a saucepan over a low heat. Cover and leave until all the bitter juices from the kidneys come out, about 10 minutes. Remove the kidneys and transfer them to a sieve (strainer). Leave them to drain for at least 20 minutes.

Meanwhile, melt the lard and fry the onion gently for about 10 minutes. Add the tomatoes, cover and simmer gently for about 15 minutes, or until the tomatoes are coming apart.

Add the kidneys and stir together. Stir in the wine and allow the alcohol to boil off, then add salt and pepper and stir again.

Simmer for about 5 minutes, then transfer on to a warm dish and sprinkle with the parsley. Serve at once.

Trippa alla Trasteverina

Tripe Stew

This has always been, and still is, a Saturday dish served in the Roman taverns and *trattorias* in the Trastevere district. It is very much appreciated by the locals, who consider this a great delicacy. If you have never tried tripe before, I should warn you that is does have a flavour very much of its own, and not everybody takes to it.

Serves 4 to 6

1kg/2lb ready cooked tripe (as bought
    from the butcher), cut into thin strips
salt
2 carrots, whole
2 sticks celery, whole
1 large onion, peeled whole
1 sprig fresh parsley
6 tablespoons sauce from Garofolato (page
    29)
3 tablespoons freshly grated pecorino
    cheese
2 tablespoons freshly grated Parmesan
    cheese
8 fresh mint leaves, chopped

Put the tripe strips into a large pan of salted water with the vegetables and the parsley. Boil for about 45 minutes, then drain and discard the vegetables and the parsley.

Place the tripe in another saucepan with the Garofolato sauce and simmer very slowly, covered, for about 20 minutes, until the tripe is tender. Remove from the heat, stir in the cheeses and the mint leaves. Serve at once.

Animelle al Prosciutto

Sweetbreads with Prosciutto

It is a tradition of Roman cuisine that sweetbreads cooked this way should always be mixed with a dish of peas or artichokes which have been simply cooked by braising them in butter. Both dishes are cooked separately and only combined at the time of serving. Please make sure your sweetbreads are pure white when you start to cook them, or you will spoil the appearance of the dish.

Serves 4 to 6

400g/14oz veal sweetbreads, well trimmed
75g/3oz prosciutto crudo (Parma ham),
    finely chopped
1 onion, peeled and sliced
salt and freshly milled black pepper
4 tablespoons sweet Marsala wine
25g/1oz/2 tablespoons butter

Put the sweetbreads in a saucepan and cover with cold water. Bring to the boil, then remove the sweetbreads and peel them quickly while they are still hot. Rinse them very thoroughly in cold water, and keep them in water until required.

Fry the ham and the onion together for about 5 minutes. Cut the sweetbreads into thick slices and add them to the pan. Season with salt and pepper and stir in the Marsala. Cook for about 12 minutes, gently stirring frequently.

Remove the sweetbreads from the pan with a slotted spoon and arrange on a warm dish. Add the butter to the pan and stir it carefully into the remaining liquid over a medium heat, scraping the bottom of the pan very thoroughly. Pour the sauce over the sweetbreads and serve at once.

Peperoni in Padella
Pan-fried Peppers

Peppers grown in the south of Italy are always incredibly sweet, juicy and enormous in size. There is something verging on the vaguely erotic about this amazing vegetable, which comes into its own when cooked with utmost simplicity as here. These peppers can be served hot or cold.

Serves 4

4 large peppers, any colour or a mixture of colours
4 tablespoons olive oil
I very large onion, peeled and sliced
4 canned tomatoes, drained, seeded and coarsely chopped
salt and freshly milled black pepper

Spear the peppers on long-handled forks and hold them over a flame, turning them around so the outer skins blacken and blister all over. Work in batches, if necessary. Rub off all the skin with a cloth, using a small knife to help with the more difficult strips.

Cut the peppers in half once they are peeled and remove all the inner seeds and membranes. Rinse them carefully, and pat dry, then cut them into large chunky pieces.

Heat the oil in a large frying pan (skillet) and fry the onion until soft. Add the peppers and the tomatoes and season with salt and pepper. Cover and simmer gently for about 10 minutes, or until the peppers are soft, stirring occasionally. Remove from the heat.

Broccoletti in Padella
Pan-fried Turnip Tops

One of the most basic recipes from the Roman countryside, using the poorest of ingredients. If turnip tops prove impossible to find, sprouting broccoli or spinach can be used instead.

Serves 4 to 6

1.5kg/3lb turnip tops, picked over, well rinsed and dried
salt
3 cloves garlic, lightly crushed
½ dried red chilli pepper
3–5 tablespoons olive oil

Remove any hard stalks (stems) and coarse leaves from the turnip leaves. Bring a large pan of generously salted water to a rolling boil. Toss in the turnip tops, stir, return to the boil and cook until tender. Drain well.

Meanwhile, fry the garlic and the chilli in a frying pan (skillet) with the oil for 5 or 6 minutes. Add the turnip tops and toss together with 2 forks for about 8 minutes, making sure the flavoured oil coats and soaks into the vegetables thoroughly. Serve either hot or cold.

Pizza di Polenta/Polenta Cake (page 37)

Fagiolini Stufati

Stewed Green Beans

There are all sorts of green beans available in Italy, from the long, thin Santa Anna variety, right through to the pale and stubby corallo. For this recipe, string beans are particularly good, especially if they are a little bit hard as the lengthy stewing process tenderizes them. This is excellent served hot or cold.

Serves 4

50ml/2fl oz/¼ cup olive oil
1 onion, peeled and chopped
1kg/2lb string beans, or other green beans, topped and tailed
500g/1lb/2 cups canned tomatoes, well drained, seeded and coarsely chopped
salt and freshly milled black pepper
3 tablespoons chopped fresh parsley

Heat the oil in a large deep frying pan (skillet) and fry the onion until soft and transparent. Add the beans and stir together, then add the tomatoes and stir again. Season to taste with salt and pepper, cover and simmer slowly until the beans are soft, about 20 to 40 minutes. Stir frequently and add a little water every now and again to keep everything moist and tender.

Just before serving, stir in the parsley.

Carciofi alla Romana

Artichokes with Mint

A classic of Roman cuisine, this is wonderful eaten either hot or cold. No other recipe, in my opinion, quite sets off the unique flavour of this vegetable quite like this one.

Serves 8

50g/2oz/1 cup chopped fresh parsley
10 leaves fresh mint, finely chopped
2 cloves garlic, finely chopped
9 tablespoons olive oil
8 globe artichokes
salt and freshly milled black pepper

Pre-heat the oven to 160°C/325°F/Gas Mark 3.

Put the chopped herbs into a bowl with the garlic and 3 tablespoons of the olive oil. Leave to stand while you prepare the artichokes.

Cut an artichoke stalk (stem) to 5cm/2in below the base. Carefully remove all the hard exterior leaves with a sharp knife. Peel the remaining section of stalk. Pull open the artichoke at the centre and scoop out the hairy choke. Snip any sharp ends off with scissors. Repeat with the remaining artichokes. Rinse and dry the artichokes inside and out with great care. Place a little of the herb and garlic mixture inside each artichoke, then sprinkle inside and out with salt and pepper and place them upside down in a deep ovenproof dish. Mix the remaining oil with 175ml/6fl oz/¾ cup water and pour it all over the artichokes, depending upon the size and shape of the dish, they should be just covered by the liquid.

Cover the dish with a lid or with foil and bake for about 1 hour. Serve the artichokes hot or cold.

Pizza Dolce di Civitavecchia

Civitavecchia Cake

You need to start making this very simple cake the day before, as the dough rises throughout the night. Altogether the dough rises three times.

Serves 6

50g/2oz fresh yeast
400g/14oz/heaped 3 cups plain white (all-purpose) flour
6 egg yolks, beaten
150g/5oz/¾ cup sugar
50g/2oz/¼ cup ricotta cheese
3 tablespoons light rum
7 egg whites, beaten until stiff
grated rind (peel) of 1 lemon
½ teaspoon ground cinnamon
½ teaspoon caraway seeds
125g/4oz/½ cup lard, diced
3 tablespoons sunflower seed oil for greasing
1 egg yolk, beaten, for brushing over the cake
3 tablespoons icing (confectioners') sugar, sifted, for dusting the cake

Dilute the yeast in about 3 tablespoons of warm water and mix into 125g/4oz/1 cup of the flour to make a small ball of dough. Place in a lightly greased bowl, cover with a cloth and leave at room temperature to rise overnight.

The next day, beat the egg yolks with the sugar until pale and light, then beat in the ricotta the rum and lemon rind. Beat the egg whites, fold them into the mixture, then carefully mix in the cinnamon and the caraway seeds.

Put the risen ball of dough on the worktop. Add the remaining flour and rub in the lard. Knead everything together very thoroughly. Slowly blend the egg mixture into the dough. Place the dough in a bowl, cover with a cloth and leave to rise until doubled in volume, about 2 hours.

Remove the dough from the bowl, knock it back and put it into a lightly greased 27.5cm/11in round cake pan. Put back in a warm place to rise for the third time, for about 30 minutes.

Pre-heat the oven to 160°C/325°F/Gas Mark 3. Brush the surface of the dough with the beaten egg yolk and dust with the icing (confectioners') sugar. Bake for about 45 minutes, until golden and firm. Cool in the pan, then turn out on to a platter to serve.

Pizza di Polenta

Polenta Cake

This is probably one of the oldest and most traditional recipes from the Lazio countryside, using very humble and simple ingredients. Every tiny village and small town in the Lazio has its own variation on this basic cake.

Makes 1 cake; serves 6–8

25g/1oz/2 tablespoons sultanas (golden raisins)
250g/8oz/1 cup ricotta cheese
125g/4oz/heaped ½ cup granulated sugar
250g/8oz/1½ cups fine polenta flour
1 teaspoon ground cinnamon
vegetable oil for greasing

Cover the sultanas (golden raisins) with warm water and leave to soak for no longer than 15 minutes, drain them and carefully pat them dry.

Meanwhile, pre-heat the oven to 150°C/300°F/Gas Mark 2. Grease a 23.75cm/9½in quiche dish. Dilute the ricotta with 500ml/¾ pint/2 cups tepid water, beating vigorously with a balloon whisk. Beat in the sugar, then add the polenta flour in a fine stream very gradually to avoid lumps. Add the cinnamon and the sultanas and give the batter one final stir. Pour the batter into the prepared dish and bang the pan on the worktop to remove any air bubbles. Bake for about 1 hour, or until the cake is firm and a knife inserted into the centre comes out clean. Serve tepid or cool, straight from the dish.

Pasticcio di Gnocchi

Gnocchi Pie

Like many of the dishes of Rome and the Lazio, this can hardly be described as a light dessert! However, it is amazingly good, very warming and rib sticking on a cold day, and certainly authentic.

Serves 6

for the pastry:
450g/1lb/heaped 3 cups plain white (all-purpose) flour
200g/7oz/1 cup sugar
125g/4oz/½ cup butter, diced
125g/4oz/½ cup lard, diced
1 egg, plus 1 extra yolk
¼ teaspoon ground cinnamon
¼ teaspoon grated nutmeg
grated rind (peel) of 1 lemon
sunflower oil for greasing

for the filling:
4 egg yolks
50g/2oz/½ cup icing (confectioners') sugar
40g/1½oz/5 tablespoons cornflour (cornstarch)
300ml/10fl oz/1¼ cups milk
25g/1oz/¼ cup plain white (all-purpose) flour
½ teaspoon grated nutmeg
½ teaspoon ground cinnamon
grated rind (peel) of 1 lemon

First make the pastry. Pile all the flour into the centre of the worktop. Make a hole in the centre with your fist, then put the sugar into the hole with the butter and the lard. Add the whole egg, the egg yolk, the spices and the lemon rind (peel). Knead together until you have a soft, round ball of dough. Wrap in clingfilm and chill for about 30 minutes.

Grease a 25cm/10in quiche dish very thoroughly. Roll out the dough and use it to line the pie dish. Chill again until required.

Now make the filling. Beat the 4 egg yolks until pale and fluffy with the icing (confectioners') sugar. Add the cornflour (cornstarch) and the milk and flour very gradually, beating constantly. Finally, stir in the spices and the grated lemon rind (peel). Pour this mixture into the lined quiche dish and bake for about 25–35 minutes at 160°/325°F/Gas Mark 3 or until golden and firm. Cool and serve from the dish.

The
Abruzzi

The Abruzzi

Of all the southern regions, the Abruzzi is the one most dominated by mountain ranges. Almost the entire region, except for the rigidly straight 120 kilometre coastal strip, consists of mountains and hills cut by deep green valleys. The climate is mild and gentle along the coast, while the inland areas are hot and dry in the summer, snow driven and bitterly cold during the long winter months.

The main city is L'Aquila, meaning the eagle, perched symbolically on a high mountain peak. This is a peaceful, attractive old town, with cobbled streets, tiny little piazzas, discreet courtyards and the grand houses of the sheep trading families all contributing to give it a very distinguished air.

In the old days the arrival of chilly autumn evenings meant that the local shepherds were about to be despatched southwards by their masters. From L'Aquila, the huge flocks went up over the mountains and down into Molise, wending their way to the greener meadows and more clement temperatures of Puglia. The long journey, known as the Transumanza, would take several months and end at Lecce, the graceful, ochre-tinted city right down in southern Puglia. This was where one of the most important sheep markets would take place, attracting merchants, farmers and traders from all parts of Italy and even from abroad. In spring and summer the flocks would make the return journey to the Abruzzi.

The long sheep trail was a way of life, not just for those directly involved in the Transumanza, but for all those living anywhere along its route. The men who travelled southwards through the winter months left a whole series of culinary traditions behind them, and a certain amount of recipe and ingredient trading was inevitable in the course of their travels. Thus, influences from Puglia, Molise and the rest of the south have filtered into the local recipes, as well as many that have their origins further afield. Mutton, kid, goat and lamb appear on the menu in restaurants and in people's houses throughout the Abruzzi. Naturally enough, although most of the sheep were bred and sold for their wool, a few were destined for the pot, and there were others that died of natural causes on the way. Under the rules of the Transumanza, no shepherd was permitted to kill and eat a single animal along the route. The flocks and the shepherds were checked night and day by the guards on horseback, who rode up and down the endless droves of sheep and men. The punishment for taking one of the master's animals was always very harsh. Yet, when occasionally a sheep *did* die of natural causes, the shepherds would sometimes be rewarded for their loyalty by being allowed to roast the poor beast on a scented wood fire.

Because the winters are long and arduous in these mountain settlements, pork has a place in the kitchen alongside the ubiquitous lamb and mutton. The most warming pork casserole I have ever come across is a dish called *N'docca n'docca* which contains large quantities of pig offal. The rest of the animal would traditionally be transformed into *salumi*, cured meats such as salame of various kinds, sausages and ham. These, accompanied by pasta and bread, would see the local families through those snowy days, and they could easily be transported by the shepherds on their travels through the winter.

The Abruzzi is respected throughout Italy for producing more expert cooks than any other region of the country. It is said that the natives of the region have an in-bred instinct for cooking, and in the catering trade in Italy they always say that any restaurant which has an Abruzzese in the kitchen cannot possibly fail. They have a certain sophistication and elegance about their cuisine which is really quite remarkable considering how relatively inaccessible this area has always been.

The very remoteness of the region has left it with a highly individual culinary tradition. Even in one of those old, grand sheep traders' houses, in a vast and amazingly well-equipped kitchen, you cannot get away from the all-pervading sense of rustic charm.

You will see, for example, the *chitarra*, the most typical and best known of Abruzzi's cookery gadgets. This is a rectangular box about the size of a large shoe box, with steel strings stretched right across it at narrow, regular intervals. The instrument needs tuning before you can begin, which is done by loosening or tightening the strings just as on a real guitar. Once the guitar is ready, the cook lays a sheet of thick hand-made pasta dough across the strings, and then rolls it with her rolling pin. Under pressure, the steel strings slice through the dough and the pasta falls into the box in the form of square, thick spaghetti.

I must tell you that this operation requires a great deal of energy and muscle power, not to mention stamina, with plenty of invocations to the blessed St Bernard. No wonder the locals used to urge their daughters to take up the job of preparing the household's pasta as they reached puberty. The theory was that making the pasta would develop the bust splendidly, so that a girl armed with the skill of pasta making, and a beautifully modelled chest, would have no trouble whatsoever in finding a good husband.

Then there are the wafer-thin little biscuits, called *ferratelle*, made in something that looks rather like a waffle iron. Once the thin batter is poured into the iron, it is held over the flame and a Hail Mary is quickly whispered. In the time it takes for the prayer to be said, the *Ferratella* is ready.

This is also the region of magic and superstition, where the strange world of spells and incantations has its place in the kitchen as well as everywhere else. Although religious belief is very strong in the Abruzzi, it seems to exist in perfect harmony alongside less orthodox and decidedly mystical beliefs. Only here will you discover cooks who stir their soups for a specific number of times and only in one direction, who pick certain herbs or vegetables for specific dishes only when the moon is full, and who whisper special prayers during the cooking process of some of their dishes.

In particular, local cooks appear to have an ongoing love affair with *il diavolicchio*, the dried red chilli pepper which they are fondly and liberally sprinkling into soups, stews and especially their pasta sauces. The dried red chilli pepper holds a position of enormous importance all over the south. It used to be considered to be a cure for everything from malaria to intestinal worms, but here in the Abruzzi, although it is used in far smaller quantities, it takes on a mysterious significance of its own.

Superstitious as they are, the Abruzzesi are also tremendously gentle, friendly people. They will overwhelm you with their hospitality! Their most impressive traditional feast is the Panarda, where approximately thirty courses are served to a gathering of family and friends seated on either side of a very long table, and where nobody can leave until all the food is eaten.

To restore a level of wellbeing after such a feast, a glass of the local liqueur is the only answer. Centerbe is not only a delicious herbal drink which settles an overworked digestive system pleasantly, it is also at the heart of a popular local story.

The Toro family have been making the drink from a secret recipe for approximately two hundred years. Made from herbs which are gathered in the mountains (although there are probably not a hundred herbs, as the name implies), it was produced at home in the kitchen by the original Toro family, loaded up on to carts and taken by road to Naples, where it was peddled on the streets as a cure for the plague and other less lethal diseases. Naturally, the Neopolitans were prepared to try anything to rid themselves of this terrible disease, and handed over large amounts of cash and jewellery. And so the Toros grew rich.

Several generations later, around 1870, Mr and Mrs Toro had reached the kind of security that only money can buy. Their daughter was of marrying age and they needed to find her a husband. If she was to attract the right sort of man

and continue the Toro family's rise in society, they needed to build an impressive family home. On a trip to Rome, Mr Toro somehow managed to acquire a recently rejected design for the new Italian embassy in Brussels. A different design had been chosen and the rejected plans were going cheap.

Once built, this became the new Toro residence and factory. It is the most extraordinary sight, this amazingly grandiose *palazzo* situated in the main street of a tiny village called Tocco Causaria in the province of Pescara. There is nobody living there anymore, except for a couple of people who continue to make the drink and look after the house. As you meander among the colonnaded pathways, and admire the incredible view of Abruzzi's most adored mountain, La Maiella, you cannot help but wonder about the Toro family and their amazing drink.

The saddest part of the story is that the house had the very opposite of the desired effect. There *was* an engagement, but apparently the house, which is indeed very big and imposing despite the fact that it is somewhat dilapidated and abandoned, blocked the prospective in-laws' view of the mountain, and a row ensued which meant that the marriage never did take place.

By contrast there is another local family-run business which is a great deal more active and where the people involved are desperately keen to carry on working. These are the saffron growers of the tiny village of Navelli. The saffron of Navelli is supposed to be the finest saffron grown anywhere and constantly wins the blind tastings carried out by the Food and Agricultural Organization's official envoy.

Saffron was first planted here by a Jesuit priest from this village who spent some time as an inquisitor in Spain and brought the crocus flower back with him as a souvenir for his farmer brother, who grew it with tremendous success. It would seem that the fertile Navelli valley has the most perfect climatic conditions for this tender flower.

I don't know if Silvio Sarra, who runs the saffron co-operative of Navelli, is in any way related to the original Jesuit monk's brother, but it would be hard to find a farmer anywhere who was quite so passionate about his crop. Silvio knows everything there is to know about saffron, from its original uses in India to all its various medicinal properties: it helps to soothe swollen gums, relieves many menstrual problems, can be used either as a relaxant or a stimulant depending upon the dose in which it is administered, lowers cholesterol levels and can affect your blood pressure. Silvio even makes his own drink out of the stuff, a strange tasting brilliant yellow concoction which is 37 degrees proof!

But the most amazing thing is to watch Silvio's workforce packing the threads or the powder into tiny little paper sachets. Seated around an amazing Heath Robinson machine in a dark little room under a 40 watt light bulb, they work incredibly hard for such a tiny profit. According to Silvio, six million lire's worth (approximately £3,000) of his saffron is consumed in Italy each year — it hardly seems worth all the trouble. For Silvio, clearly, it is a labour of love, and I for one will never again begrudge the high price tag which comes with every gramme of this exquisite spice.

If I had to name one quintessential gastronomic symbol for this region it would have to be the ubiquitous dried red chilli pepper, which seems to pervade every kitchen with its inimitable scent. Though the doses in which it is used here are not breathtaking, as they are in other regions of the south like Calabria, or even neighbouring Molise, the cooks of the Abruzzi are justly famous for their careful, measured flavouring techniques. But these cooks are also experts at preparing tender casseroles of lamb, and they have access to marvellous local cheeses, and excellent vegetables: especially artichokes, celery and cardoons, of which they are inordinately fond. Their region produces fine wines and is one of only two places in Italy where saffron is grown (the other being Sardinia).

With all this, the Abruzzese gastronomic tradition cannot fail to take its place among the best in the south, a position it would accept with the great pride that has always been the main characteristic of this region.

Cardone in Brodo con Polpette

Cardoon Soup with Meatballs

The cardoon is a very unusual, but absolutely delicious, vegetable which looks a little like celery but tastes much more like a globe artichoke. Start early in the day for this recipe, so the cardoon can soak 3 hours to lose all its bitter juices.

This recipe is typical of Abruzzese cookery, using very simple ingredients and turning the finished dish into something really quite sophisticated. It is the traditional Christmas Eve dish of the lovely little town of Chieti.

Serves 4 to 6

1 fresh cardoon, weighing about 1.5kg/3lb
juice of 2 lemons
1 teaspoon plain white (all-purpose) flour

for the meatballs:
300g/10oz minced (ground) pork
3 eggs, beaten
125g/4oz/1 cup freshly grated pecorino
    cheese
salt

for the soup:
5 eggs, beaten
200g/7oz/1¾ cups freshly grated
    Parmesan cheese
salt and freshly milled black pepper
2.25 litres/3¾ pints/9 cups chicken or
    turkey stock

Clean the cardoon with great care. Remove all the hard exterior leaves and trim off the leaves. String each stalk (stem) and remove all traces of the white, furry skin. Rinse the cardoon stalks, then cut them into small pieces. Leave them to soak in a large bowl of water with the juice of 1 lemon for about 3 hours.

Drain the cardoon pieces and place them in a saucepan with enough salted cold water to cover and the juice of the other lemon and the flour. Boil the cardoon gently until tender, about 15 or 20 minutes, depending on the thickness.

Drain the cardoon pieces and squeeze dry with your hands. Place in a bowl and set aside.

Go on to the meatballs. Mix the pork with the eggs and the pecorino. Season with salt. Roll small amounts of the mixture between your palms to make little meatballs no bigger than cherries. Set aside until required.

Beat the 5 eggs into the cardoons, then add the Parmesan. Arrange this mixture at the bottom of a deep saucepan. Pour over the stock and add in the raw meatballs. Cover the saucepan and bring it to the boil, then simmer for about 5 minutes, or until the meatballs are cooked through. Serve at once.

Polenta al Forno

Baked Polenta

A deliciously filling dish of polenta which is sliced and then layered in a dish with a rich sausage ragù and sliced scamorza cheese. This is a simpler and considerably cheaper version of traditional lasagne. But still allow at least a whole day to make.

Serves 4

for the sauce:
2 tablespoons olive oil
1 onion, peeled and chopped
2 cloves garlic, chopped
1 stick celery, chopped
1 carrot, scraped and chopped
6 Italian sausages
750g/1½lb/3 cups tomato passata
salt and freshly milled black pepper

for the polenta:
2 litres/2 quarts cold water
2 tablespoons coarse sea salt
1 tablespoon olive oil
500g/1lb/3 cups coarse polenta flour

to finish off the dish:
125g/4oz/1 cup freshly grated piquant
    pecorino cheese
3 scamorza cheeses, sliced thinly

Make the sauce first. Fry the oil, onion, garlic, celery and carrot together gently until all the vegetables are soft. Prick the sausages all over and fry them gently in the same pan with the vegetables all over until the fat begins to run freely. When the sausages are browned, add the passata and stir thoroughly. Season with salt and freshly milled black pepper, cover and simmer for about 2 hours, stirring frequently.

Take the sausages out of the sauce and slice them thinly. Set the sliced sausages and the sauce to one side.

Now maked the polenta.

Bring 2 litres/2 quarts water to a rolling boil with the salt and the oil. Slowly and very gradually trickle in the polenta flour, stirring quickly and constantly all the time to prevent lumps forming.

If you use quick-cook polenta, you will only need to cook it, stirring constantly, for a further 5 minutes. Traditional polenta flour will require 50 minutes of constantly stirring, before it is ready.

When the polenta comes away from the sides of the saucepan easily, tip it out on to a board and leave it to cool completely. When the polenta is cold, slice it into thin strips. Meanwhile, pre-heat the oven to 200°C/400°F/Gas Mark 6.

Cover the bottom of an ovenproof dish large enough to take all the ingredients with some of the sauce. Then add a layer of sliced polenta and a layer of both grated and sliced cheese. Finally, add a layer of sliced sausages and cover with more sauce. Repeat until all the ingredients have been used up. Finish off with a layer of grated pecorino. Bake for about 25 minutes. Serve very hot.

Zuppa di Lenticchie Abruzzese

Abruzzese Lentil Soup

Lentils from this region are famous all over Italy for their flavour and appearance (they are tiny, smooth and brown). The most special ones of all are the ones grown in the province of l'Aquila, at Santo Stefano di Sessanio.

This marvellously nourishing soup is a speciality of the beautiful city of l'Aquila. If you use the authentic tiny, brown, very hard lentils, they will need to be soaked overnight first, whereas the more common orange or green lentils can be cooked without soaking. You can also substitute dried lentils for the canned variety.

Serves 4 to 6

200g/7oz/1 cup of dried brown lentils
2 cloves garlic, finely chopped
75ml/3fl oz/5 tablespoons olive oil
salt and freshly milled black pepper

Cover the lentils in cold water and leave them to soak overnight.

The next day, skim off any which might be floating on the surface, then drain and rinse the rest. Place the lentils in a saucepan, cover with cold water and bring to a rolling boil for 5 minutes, then drain and rinse again. Set aside.

Fry the garlic in the oil in a deep saucepan for 5 minutes, then add the lentils and stir together thoroughly. Pour in about 1.98 litres/3½ pints/8¾ cups cold water. Cover and bring to the boil, then simmer for 1 hour, or until the lentils are pulpy. Season with salt and freshly milled black pepper and serve at once.

Pizza Rustica

Rustic Pizza Pie

Not a pizza in the usual sense, this is actually a pie with a rich cheesy filling, rather than a thin disc of bread dough with a topping. It is delicious, and perfect to take on picnics.

Serves 6 to 8

extra butter for greasing
extra flour for dusting

for the pastry:
300g/10oz/2½ cups plain white (all-purpose) flour
125g/4oz/½ cup butter, cubed
2 eggs
1 egg yolk
salt

for the filling:
200g/7oz cooked ham, chopped
300g/10oz mozzarella cheese, sliced
2 eggs, beaten
4 tablespoons freshly grated Parmesan cheese

Pre-heat the oven to 220°C/425°F/Gas Mark 7.

Make the pastry (dough) first. Pile all the flour on the worktop and make a hollow in the centre with your fist. Put the cubed butter, the eggs and the egg yolk into the hollow. Add a pinch of salt and knead everything together until you have a smooth, soft ball of dough. Divide the pastry roughly in half. Roll out the larger piece on to a floured surface until it is big enough to line a buttered 27.5cm/11in quiche dish. Prick the pastry all over the bottom with a fork. Roll out the second piece of dough until it is big enough to make a lid for the pie.

Scatter the ham all over the bottom of the pastry case. Scatter the mozzarella over the ham. Pour most of the beaten eggs over the ham and mozzarella, reserving a little bit to brush over the finished pie. Sprinkle the grated Parmesan all over and finally place the second piece of pastry dough on top of the filling.

Seal the edges very carefully by pinching them together, then brush the remaining egg all over the lid. Bake for about 25 minutes, or until golden brown. Serve just warm but not too hot.

Pizza Rustica/Rustic Pizza Pie

Calzoncini Abruzzesi

Ricotta Fritters

One glance at this recipe will tell you that this is a very filling and hearty antipasto dish, not a delicate little starter (appetizer) designed to merely tickle your taste-buds! Traditionally, in fact, this is served as part of a great mound of deep-fried goodies, such as artichoke hearts, scamorza cheese, brain, cauliflower florets (flowerets) and many other delicious bits and pieces. This would then be followed by the pasta course, the main course, the desserts . . . I have been to some feasts in the Abruzzi where we sat down to eat at 1 o'clock in the afternoon and did not get up again until 7 o'clock in the evening!!

Makes about 16

flour for dusting
vegetable oil for deep-frying

for the filling:
300g/10oz/2¼ cups ricotta cheese
2 egg yolks
125g/4oz prosciutto crudo (Parma ham),
    finely chopped
125g/4oz/1 cup provolone cheese,
    coarsely grated
50g/2oz/1 cup chopped fresh parsley
salt and freshly milled black pepper

for the pastry:
400g/14oz/heaped 3 cups plain white
    (all-purpose) flour
2 eggs
125g/4oz/½ cup lard, diced
juice of 1 lemon
salt

Make the filling first. Mix all the ingredients together, stirring until you have reduced this to a smooth, even consistency.

Now make the pastry (dough). Pile the flour on the worktop and make a hollow in the centre with your fist. Break the eggs into the hole, then add the lard, lemon juice and a pinch of salt. Knead it all together until you have a smooth ball of dough.

Roll out the pastry on a floured surface, then cut into 7cm/3in circles using a biscuit (cookie) cutter. Put a spoonful of the filling on one half of each circle, then fold in half and seal tightly closed by pressing the prongs of a fork all the way around the open edge.

Heat the oil until a small piece of bread dropped into it sizzles instantly. Slide the *calzoncini* into the oil, about 4 at a time, and fry them on both sides until puffy and golden, about 5 minutes. Drain well on kitchen paper (paper towels) and keep warm until they have all been fried. Serve piping hot.

Scrippelle in Brodo

Pancakes in Chicken Broth

A very filling dish, deliciously warming on snow-bound evenings. It is imperative that the chicken stock is really bursting with flavour, for this dish to be successful.

Serves 4 to 6

4 eggs, beaten

2 tablespoons milk

3 tablespoons chopped fresh parsley

1 tablespoon freshly grated Parmesan
cheese

¼ teaspoon salt

¼ teaspoon grated nutmeg

3 tablespoons plain white (all-purpose)
flour

1.35 litres/2¼ pints/5½ cups very good-
quality chicken stock

2 tablespoons lard

75g/3oz/¾ cup freshly grated Parmeasn
cheese

Beat the eggs with the milk, parsley, Parmesan, salt
and nutmeg. Gradually beat in the flour, then
dilute the batter with 2–3 tablespoons water. You
should end up with a batter that has the
consistency of uncooked meringue.

Bring the stock to the boiling point and keep it
hot. Grease a 10cm/5in frying pan (skillet) with
lard and heat until sizzling hot. Fry a small amount
of the batter in the pan to make a very thin
pancake (crêpe). Turn it over and cook it on the
other side, then remove it from the pan and roll it
up. Continue until all the batter has been used up,
keeping the pancakes hot.

When you are ready to serve, arrange 2 or 3
pancakes in each person's soup bowl and sprinkle
generously with grated cheese. Pour over the
boiling hot stock to cover, then serve at once.

Spaghetti al Sugo d'Agnello e Peperoni

Spaghetti with Lamb and Pepper Sauce

A classical Abruzzese speciality with a very sweet,
rich flavour. You can, of course, use any shape of
pasta you like, not just spaghetti.

Serves 4

200g/7oz lean, boneless lamb, cubed

salt and freshly milled black pepper

3–4 cloves garlic, crushed

4 tablespoons olive oil

4 tablespoons dry red wine

4 canned tomatoes, drained, seeded and
chopped

2 large peppers, seeded, cored and sliced
into strips

400g/14oz spaghetti

Season the meat thoroughly with salt and pepper.
Fry the garlic with the oil in a saucepan for about
2 minutes. Add the meat and brown it all over, then
stir in the wine. Simmer for about 10 minutes, then
stir in the tomatoes and the peppers. Cover and
leave to simmer, stirring occasionally, for about
2 hours. If the sauce appears to be drying out, add
a little water.

When the meat in the sauce is tender, bring a
large pan of salted water to a rolling boil. Toss in
the spaghetti stir, return to the boil and cook until
just tender, about 7 minutes depending on the
brand. Drain and return to the pan, pour over the
sauce and toss everything together. Transfer to a
warm bowl and serve at once.

Strengozze

Fresh Pasta with Mutton Sauce

A characteristic Abruzzese sheep farmer's dish, this
is very strongly flavoured. The pasta is cut roughly,
and the rich mutton sauce is set off by peppery
pecorino cheese. You can, of course, use the sauce
to dress any kind of pasta you like.

Serves 4 to 5

extra flour for dusting
5 tablespoons freshly grated pecorino
   cheese to garnish

for the sauce:
10 fresh rosemary leaves
1 onion, peeled and sliced
50g/2oz/¼ cup lard
300g/10oz boneless mutton, cubed
150ml/5fl oz dry white wine
400g/14oz/1¾ cups canned tomatoes,
   seeded and chopped
salt and freshly milled black pepper

for the pasta:
350g/12oz/2¾ cups plain white (all-
   purpose) flour
salt

Make the sauce first. Chop the rosemary, lard and
onion together thoroughly. Fry the lard mixture in
a saucepan until the onion is soft and transparent,
then add the mutton and brown it thoroughly on
all sides. Add the wine and boil off the alcohol for
about 2 minutes, then stir in the tomatoes. Season
and cover. Leave to simmer for about 1½ hours.

Meanwhile, make the pasta. Pile the flour on
the worktop and make a hollow in the centre with
your fist. Add a little water and begin to knead
them together, working in more water until you
achieve a pliable dough. Knead energetically until
the dough is elastic enough to roll out. Roll out
the dough on a floured surface and cut it all
into uneven shapes. Leave it to dry out on a
floured surface.

When the sauce is ready, bring a large pan of
salted water to a rolling boil. Toss in the pasta, stir,
return to the boil and cook until just tender, for
about 6 minutes, depending upon the size of the
shapes. Drain it and return to the saucepan. Pour
over the sauce and toss together. Transfer to a
warm bowl, sprinkle with the cheese and serve at
once.

Pasta e Fagioli con Zampini e Codini

Pasta and Beans with Pig's Trotter and Tails

A very rustic soup, perfect for cold winter days!
Start the day before as the beans will need to soak
overnight.

Serves 4

125g/4oz/⅔ cup dried cannellini beans
1 bay leaf
1 pig's trotter, prepared by the butcher and
   ready to cook
2 pig's tails, prepared by the butcher and
   ready to cook
salt and freshly milled black pepper
200g/7oz/1 cup small tube-shaped pasta,
   such as tubetti

Cardi al Formaggio / Cardoons with Cheese (page 57)

Cover the beans with tepid water and leave to soak overnight.

The next day, drain and rinse them, then put them in a saucepan. Cover with fresh cold water and bring to a rolling boil for 5 minutes, then drain and rinse again.

Return the beans to the saucepan and cover with fresh water. Add the bay leaf and simmer very slowly for about 1 hour, or until completely tender.

Meanwhile, boil the pig's trotter and tails in plenty of water for 10 minutes, then drain and chop them into small sections, discarding all bone and gristle. Put them back into the saucepan and cover them with fresh water. Add 2 pinches of salt and simmer slowly for about 45 minutes.

As the pork cooks, pour some of the stock from the meat into the beans. When both the beans and the pork are cooked, remove the pork from the heat and remove the meat with a slotted spoon. Set the meat aside and strain the stock carefully.

Return the stock to the boil and cook the pasta in it for about 10 minutes, or until tender. Add the meat and the beans, heat through thoroughly for about 5 minutes, then add plenty of freshly milled black pepper. Serve at once.

Agnello All'Abruzzese

Spicy Lamb Casserole

Lamb and mutton are the meats most cooked in this region, in a thousand and one delicious ways. This is one of my favourite recipes, which I think best typifies the local rustic style of cooking. Ideally the lamb should be five or six months old.

Serves 4 to 6

1.2kg/2lb 10oz lean, boneless leg of lamb, cubed
9 tablespoons olive oil
1 dried red chilli pepper, chopped
3 cloves garlic, chopped
1 large onion, peeled and chopped
1 large glass dry white wine
6 cloves
20 button onions, peeled
1kg/2lb fresh tomatoes, peeled, seeded and chopped
500g/1lb peppers, seeded, cored and sliced into strips
salt and freshly milled black pepper

Rinse and pat dry the meat. Pour about half of the oil into a flameproof casserole and fry the chilli, garlic and onion gently for about 10 minutes, until soft. Add the meat and brown it all over. Stir in the wine and boil off the alcohol for about 2 minutes, then add enough warm water to cover the meat. Place a lid on the casserole and simmer the meat very gently for 1 hour.

Insert the cloves into 6 of the button onions, then add all the onions to the casserole and season. Stir in the tomatoes, cover and simmer for a further 1 hour.

In a separate pan, fry the peppers in the remaining oil for about 10 minutes. When they are softened, tip them into the lamb stew and stir carefully. Cover and cook for a further 10 minutes before serving.

Involtini con Fagioli

Stuffed Veal Rolls with Beans

This is a typical, special occasion Abruzzese speciality, using lots of varied ingredients in a style of cooking which is both imaginative and sophisticated.

Serves 4

12 thin veal escalopes (scallops), each weighing about 50g/2oz, well trimmed
2 tablespoons plain white (all-purpose) flour
5 tablespoons sunflower oil
50g/2oz ham fat removed from prosciutto crudo (Parma ham)
500g/1lb canned butter beans, well drained
500g/1lb fresh ripe tomatoes, peeled and seeded

for the filling:
125g/4oz/1½ cups fresh mushrooms, peeled and finely sliced
3 tablespoons olive oil
6 tablespoons chopped fresh parsley
5 cloves garlic, peeled and chopped
125g/4oz minced (ground) pork
125g/4oz minced (ground) veal
75g/3oz/¾ cup freshly grated Parmesan cheese
1 egg, beaten
salt and freshly milled black pepper

To make the filling, put the mushrooms into a saucepan with the olive oil, one-third of the parsley and 2 cloves of chopped garlic. Season, stir and simmer gently until the mushrooms are tender and all their liquid has evaporated, about 8 minutes. Put aside to cool.

Mix together the minced (ground) pork and veal. Blend in the cooled mushrooms, the cheese, the egg and half the remaining parsley. Season to taste and shape the mixture into 12 sausage-shaped rolls.

Flatten the veal escalopes (scallops) and arrange 1 roll of filling in the centre of each. Roll up each veal escalope and tie it closed securely with string. Dust the veal rolls with flour.

Heat the sunflower oil in a large frying pan (skillet) and fry the floured veal rolls all over until golden brown. Set aside until required.

Fry the remaining garlic and parsley with the ham fat in a separate saucepan until the garlic is soft. Add the beans and tomatoes and season to taste with salt and pepper. Simmer very gently for about 25 minutes, or until well reduced.

Lay the veal rolls in the beans and turn them frequently as you heat the whole dish through for about 10 minutes. Arrange on a warmed platter and serve at once.

Stoccafisso in Umido con Patate e Olive

Stewed Stockfish with Potatoes and Olives

Stoccafisso is very popular in Italy, and, like salt cod, must be soaked for three days in several changes of cold water before cooking.

Serves 4

900g/1lb 13oz stockfish, soaked in several
    changes of water for 3 days
2 onions, peeled and finely chopped
4 tablespoons olive oil
200g/7oz/scant 1 cup canned tomatoes,
    sieved (pushed through a strainer)
2 tablespoons chopped fresh parsley
800g/1¾lb potatoes, peeled and cut into
    ½cm/¼in slices
150g/5oz/1 cup stoned black (pitted ripe)
    olives
6 leaves fresh basil
salt and freshly milled black pepper

Rinse the fish thoroughly. Put it in a saucepan and
cover with fresh water. Boil for about 15 minutes,
then drain and cut into chunks about the same size
as the sliced potatoes. Fry the onions in the oil
until the onion is soft. Stir in the tomatoes and
parsley and simmer for about 10 minutes, then add
the fish and the potatoes. Cover and simmer for
about 15 minutes, or until the potatoes are soft,
stirring occasionally with great care so you do not
break up the potatoes. If the stew appears to be
drying out, add a little water.

    Stir in the olives and the basil and adjust
seasoning to taste. Heat through for about
5 minutes, then serve.

Patate e Peperoni Rossi

Potatoes with Red Peppers

An original and delicious way of serving
mashed potatoes. This is good as a side dish with
pork or liver, and it is delicious on its own or
with fried eggs.

Serves 4

750g/1½lb small old potatoes, even sized
    and scrubbed
salt and freshly milled black pepper
4 juicy red peppers, rinsed
1 teaspoon dried oregano
2 cloves garlic, very finely chopped
2 tablespoons chopped fresh parsley
8 tablespoons olive oil

Put the potatoes in a saucepan of cold salted water
and boil them until tender. Drain well, then peel
them quickly while they are still very hot and mash
them thoroughly with a fork.

    Meanwhile, grill (broil) the peppers all over
until the skin is blackened and the flesh feels soft.
Put the hot peppers into a plastic bag and tie it
closed loosely and leave them to cool for about
5 minutes. Take the peppers out of the bag and
peel them quickly. Remove any trace of charred
skin, then cut each in half and discard all the seeds
and membranes. Cut the peppers into neat strips
and arrange them on a warmed platter.

    Sprinkle with the oregano, garlic, parsley, salt
and pepper and olive oil. Tip the piping hot
mashed potato on top of the peppers and mix
everything together. Serve at once.

Patate e Peperoni Rossi/Potatoes and Red Peppers,
and Seppie Affogate/Squid Casserole (page 30)

Carciofi Ripieni

Stuffed Artichokes

This is a fantastic recipe for artichokes with a tuna fish stuffing.

Serves 4 as a main course or 8 as an antipasto

8 globe artichokes
juice of 1 lemon
5 salted anchovies, well rinsed, patted dry and boned
50g/2oz/⅓ cup capers, well drained
1 clove garlic, chopped
150g/5oz canned tuna, well drained and flaked
6 tablespoons olive oil

Cut off the stalks (stems) from all artichokes to 5cm/2in from the base. Remove all the hard exterior leaves from an artichoke. Pull open the artichoke at the centre and scoop out the hairy choke from inside. Snip any sharp ends off with scissors. Repeat with the remaining artichokes.

Rinse them thoroughly and drop them into a bowl of cold water with the lemon juice.

Chop the anchovies with the capers, then mix them with the garlic and the tuna. Use this mixture to fill all the artichokes.

Use half the oil to grease a flameproof dish large enough to take the artichokes in a single layer. Arrange the artichokes upright in the dish. Drizzle with the remaining olive oil, then cover and simmer slowly for about 40 minutes, or until the leaves are tender. Add a little water if the artichokes appear to be drying out too much during the cooking. Serve hot.

Patate e Lenticchie

Potatoes with Lentils

This is one of my favourite easy-to-eat meals, ideal either in winter or summer. It is a very cheap and nourishing way to feed a family deliciously!

Serves 4

150g/5oz/¾ cup dried brown or green lentils
1 stick celery, coarsely chopped
1 large carrot, chopped
1 large onion, chopped
2 cloves garlic chopped
5 tablespoons olive oil
3 rashers (sliced) pancetta or streaky bacon, chopped (optional)
1 10cm/4in sprig fresh rosemary
salt and freshly milled black pepper
4 or 5 potatoes, peeled and cubed
250ml/8fl oz/1 cup chicken or meat stock

Soak the lentils overnight in plenty of cold water.

The following day, drain and rinse the lentils thoroughly and place them in a saucepan of fresh water to cover. Bring to the boil and boil for 5 minutes, then drain and rinse again. Return to the pan and just cover with fresh cold water. Simmer for about 15 minutes, or until soft.

In a separate pan, fry together the celery, carrot, onion, garlic, olive oil, bacon and rosemary until the fat in the bacon begins to run. Add the lentils with all their liquid and stir thoroughly. Season generously, cover and simmer for about 30 minutes, stirring frequently. Add the potatoes and the stock and finish off the cooking, uncovered, until the potatoes are tender all the way through. Adjust seasoning as necessary and serve at once, with bread and salad.

Cardi al Formaggio

Cardoons with Cheese

This vegetable, which is a very close relative of the globe artichoke, is linked to various local legends, spells and rituals. Locals say that it is possible to read the future from the shape of the leaves which have been left to flower into the traditional violet blooms, but this is dependent upon whether or not you pick it on St John's night.

Serves 4

1kg/2lb cardoons
1 lemon, sliced into 6 wedges
salt and freshly milled black pepper
150g/5oz mozzarella cheese, thinly sliced
2 cloves garlic, finely chopped
4–6 tablespoons fresh white breadcrumbs
6 tablespoons olive oil
extra oil for dish

String and trim all the cardoons, carefully rubbing off all trace of white surface "fur". Cut each stalk (stem) into 4 or 5 sections. Rub them all over with lemon before dropping them into a bowl of cold water. When they are all prepared, transfer them to a saucepan and cover with fresh water. Add salt and bring to the boil, then simmer until tender. Drain well and set to one side.

Oil an ovenproof dish large enough to take all the cardoons and the cheese in a double layer, using about half the oil. Preheat the oven to 190°C/375°F/Gas Mark 5. Arrange half the cardoons in the bottom of the dish, cover with cheese and drizzle on a little oil. Scatter over the garlic and then cover with more cardoons, the remaining cheese, the breadcrumbs and finally a sprinkling of salt, pepper and the remaining oil. Bake for about 20 minutes, or until browned. Serve at once.

Piselli Cacio e Uova

Peas with Egg and Cheese

A very simple, but rather filling, recipe for fresh or frozen peas. The consistency is like that of a very wet omelette – almost a soup.

Serves 4

4 tablespoons olive oil
1 large onion, peeled and sliced
1kg/2lb fresh peas in the pod, shelled, or 450g/1lb frozen peas
300ml/½ pint/1¼ cups chicken or vegetable stock
2 eggs, beaten
4 tablespoons freshly grated Parmesan cheese
salt and freshly milled black pepper

Heat the oil in a wide frying pan (skillet) and fry the onion until soft. Add the peas and stir in the stock. Simmer gently until the peas are very tender. Stir in beaten eggs and the Parmesan. Season to taste with salt and pepper and serve at once.

Ciambelline Abruzzesi

Abruzzesi Ring Biscuits

This is one of the most basic and simple recipes for biscuits (cookies). These are deliberately firm so they can be easily dunked into wine at the end of a meal. They are also delicious when dipped into frothy, milky coffee for a very Italian breakfast!

Makes about a dozen

125g/4oz/scant ½ cup caster (superfine) sugar
125ml/4fl oz/½ cup dry or sweet red wine
125ml/4fl oz/½ cup olive oil
250g/8oz/2 cups plain white (all-purpose) flour (this is an approximate measurement as it is hard to gage the density of the oil)
1 tablespoon lard

Preheat the oven to 160°C/325°F/Gas Mark 3. Mix the sugar, wine and oil together. Beat in as much flour as required to make a pliable, kneadable texture. Place the ball of dough in a bowl, covered with a cloth and leave in a cool place to rest for at least 30 minutes.

Meanwhile, grease a baking sheet with the lard. Roll out the dough, then cut it into 10cm/4in long cylindrical strips. Bend the strips into rings and lay all the rings on the baking sheet.

Bake for about 20 minutes, until golden. Cool on wire racks. Serve or store in an air-tight container.

Parozzo Abruzzese

Chocolate-covered Cake

This is reputed to be the nationalist poet Gabriele D'Annunzio's favourite cake from his beloved region.

Serves 6

75g/3oz/⅔ cup blanched almonds
125g/4oz/heaped 1 cup granulated sugar
75g/3oz/5 tablespoons unsalted butter
5 eggs, separated
50g/2oz/½ cup plain white (all-purpose) flour, sifted
50g/2oz/½ cup cornflour (cornstarch), sifted
extra butter for greasing
150g/5oz couverture chocolate

Pre-heat the oven to 180°C/350°F/Gas Mark 4. Butter a 10cm/3–4in deep cake tin (pan). Pound the almonds into a fine powder with a pestle and mortar, or use a food processor, with about one-third of the sugar. Melt the butter in the top half of a double boiler and leave to cool without hardening. Beat the egg yolks with a balloon whisk in a large mixing bowl, gradually adding the remaining sugar until they are light and fluffy.

Add the almond mixture, flour, cornflour and the butter alternately, stirring constantly. Beat the egg whites until stiff, then fold them gently into the mixture. Pour the cake batter into the tin. Bake for about 40 minutes, or until a knife inserted into the centre of the cake comes out clean. Leave to cool in the cake tin, then turn out on to a wire rack to cool completely.

Melt the chocolate until liquid, then pour it over the top of the cake to cover, using a palette knife (metal spatula) to spread it evenly. Leave the chocolate to harden, then transfer to a large plate and serve.

Molise

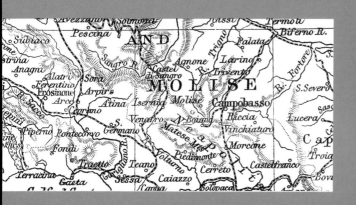

Molise

There is something infinitely romantic about this tiny little region. Just outside Campobasso, the main town, stands a cold, grey stone tower. The locals say that many hundreds of years ago a local nobleman built the tower around his lady love, encasing her for ever inside the tower. Somehow, the tower reminds me of Molise herself: there is a certain sadness, an unspoken loneliness in the air here which you just cannot escape from.

Molise was for centuries little more than a place the sheep trails of the Transumanza crossed on the way from the Abruzzi to Puglia. Apart from this, there has never been any real reason to come to Molise, and so it has largely been left to its own devices, never really catching up with the rest of the country. Despite the land reclamation programmes, the redevelopment programmes, the establishment of Molise's regional autonomy, the huge efforts which have been made in establishing the region's cultural position, Molise's main problem has been the interminable drain of human resources: large-scale emigration from this area has been going on virtually non stop since the turn of the century. Molise is too backward, too quiet, too economically unstable for her people. And so they leave her behind.

Those who do stay enjoy a kind of splendid isolation, and all those I have met have always expressed an amazing loyalty to their region and all that it produces. And you will often hear them joke about the exodus. 'Oh, yes,' they laugh, 'there are more Molisani living in Toronto now than there are right here in Molise!'

The Toronto Molisani also have a great pride, and apparently hold an annual Molisan feast in celebration of their homeland, with cooks from Molise flown in to prepare the food authentically. And what marvellous food it is! Ovid and Plinius used to sing the praises of Molise's sublime olive oil. The Transumanza and those interminable sheep droves have allowed the development of excellent ewe's milk cheeses, including a unique gooey pecorino, as well as a host of lamb and mutton recipes. The harsh winters (endless rain in November, and mountain snow which lasts until June some years) created a need for making cured pork meats to get through the cold days and nights. The most justly famous of these is the excellent soppressata sausage, and the incredibly spicy pamparella.

Delicious wines are also produced locally (albeit in very small quantities), but pride of place goes to the fantastic local pasta. Molise has always been famous for its pasta, which has a flavour and density unlike any other. Indeed, long before the famous *La Molisana* pasta factory was set up by Michele Carlone in 1912, the grain which was grown and milled here was considered to be of far superior quality to any other.

The local, traditional fresh pasta is fairly basic, consisting of simple hand-made shapes dressed with sauces made with whatever was available. It was the young ladies of high-class families who were sent away to be educated at colleges in Naples who were responsible for bringing home the skills required for making the more sophisticated pasta dishes, such as Lasagne, La Genovese and others.

The same young ladies of good breeding also brought back other recipes and ideas, which quickly became absorbed into the local gastronomy.

The superstitions, magical belief and intense religious fervour which characterize Abruzzese culture also have a firm hold on that of Molise. Yet there are local spells, incantations and proverbs which are unique to this region. Here they believe, for example, that beans (which appear in countless local recipes) are a lucky symbol, capable of warding off evil spirits and poverty, bringing good fortune and/or wealth to all those who eat them. It is fortunate that pulses at least have always been easy to cultivate in this unyielding, stony soil.

For the occasion of the feast of San Giuseppe, on 19 March, it is traditional in certain families to prepare a feast of thirteen courses – one course for each of St Joseph's virtues (honesty, kindness, generosity, gentleness etc). Everybody present is supposed to eat a little of each in order to be blessed by the occasion because St Joseph is, among other things, the Protector of Good Death, making sure that one's passage from life into death is smooth and effortless. Even if they really don't like the food, they have to eat a little of each of the thirteen courses in order to assure themselves of a smooth passage to heaven!

This is not a joyful occasion, but a religious feast of great seriousness and significance. It is a tradition carried out by the so-called *Sacre Famiglie* (holy families), those who have experienced a miracle or who at some time or another have been touched by the grace of God. The tradition is handed down from one generation to the next, no matter how many centuries ago the original miracle occurred! They cook for up to 150 people, and anybody who passes is allowed to come in, sit down and eat.

This invitation also extends to the *pezzente* (a word which translates with some difficulty, but which basically means the local beggar), who according to an obscure local custom is offered food from a blue bucket with a black handle. The bucket contains one ladleful of each of the thirteen courses. According to the local custom, one of these courses has to be an orange salad.

Apart from the feast itself, there is an extra course consisting of calzoni (crescent shaped pastries) filled with a paste of chick peas mixed with honey. Most families pride themselves on making the ultimate sacrifice for this feast by pushing the softened chick peas through the hard metal sieve with their bare hands. Others take a short cut by pounding the puree with a pestle and mortar. You can be certain of one thing: *everybody* knows who is prepared to suffer for St Joseph and who is not, and apparently these gossipy details are carefully noted by the local priest. Because of the link with St Joseph's patronage, these calzoni are also taken as gifts to bereaved families as an augury for peaceful mourning, and to hasten the departed's passage to heaven.

Molise only finally regained her independence from the Abruzzi in 1963, which is why so many of the local traditional dishes will remind you very much of the cooking of the Abruzzi. Yet there is a difference between the sophisticated recipes of the rich sheep traders of L'Aquila, and the peasant simplicity you will find here. Probably the recipe which best illustrates the sheer grinding misery which existed here for so many centuries is called *Pesce Fuiute*, or Escaped Fish. The ingredients list includes three or four small stones taken from the sea bed. These are put into the pan with olive oil, onion and tomatoes to make a simple sauce for pasta which would at least have the perfume of the sea, if not the flavour. Of fish there is no trace, as whoever thought up the recipe was obviously unable to afford it. The recipe recommends that it is best to 'fish' stones from around the reefs, as they are more flavoursome.

The people here cling on to their own gastronomy and the anecdotes and stories attached to it with a far greater passion than I have encountered elsewhere. You only need to ask someone about culinary tradition and they'll be happy to let you help make the pasta; and will probably also tell you how at the turn of the century Cascalenda was the only place where you could buy sea fish inland, and about the legendary Antonia Iacobucci from Campobasso, who can make cavatielli (the local pasta) faster than anybody: her record stands at three kilos in an hour and three-quarters.

Every saint's day, holy day and village festa is marked by ancient traditions of food and wine. And whereas in other parts of the country these ancient rituals have been forgotten or abandoned, here they are kept alive with a passion that is part of the courageous spirit of this lonely region.

Molise was united with the Abruzzi until 1963, when it finally became an autonomous region. The general history of the region follows that of the Abruzzi closely.

Of Molise's more remote history there are traces scattered throughout its territory, particularly at Pietrabbondante (the word means plenty of stone!), where the ruins of ancient temples and an amphitheatre can be seen. Archaeological excavations throughout the area have led to the discovery of ancient Samnite and Roman settlements, some of which are unique to this region. Human traces from both the palaeolithic and neolithic periods have been found throughout the region. Some of these cultures would appear to have existed here for over a millennium. The various tribes which inhabited the area were only subdued by the Romans after a very long and bitter struggle.

After the fall of the empire, the region was ruled by the dukes of Spoleto and Benevento, then taken over by the Normans, who united it with Puglia. Finally, under the Angevins, it became the responsibility of the Kingdom of Naples, and in 1684, under the Bourbons, Molise was annexed to the Abruzzi for the first time.

The region holds many surprises for the visitor, not the least of which is the fact that it is so delightfully unspoiled and unknown. Its gastronomic riches are not as famous as some of the other specialities of the south, but they are none the less impressive – perhaps more so given the remoteness of the place. There is much to discover about the cuisine of Molise, and it is worth the effort, for a great deal of love and imagination has gone into it.

Tagliolini alla Termolese/Tagliolini with Mussels and Clams (page 65), and Spaghetti con le Anguille/Spaghetti with Eels (page 70)

Zuppa della Salute

Health-giving Soup

This is the Molisan translation of the classical *zuppa santé*. It is an extremely rich and filling soup which does require a fair amount of preparation, and is therefore usually saved for Christmas festivities, or for some other special occasion.

Serves 4

2.5kg/5lb oven-ready chicken, or 2 smaller
    chickens of the same weight
4 sprigs fresh parsley
1½ teaspoons salt
300g/10oz minced (ground) beef, pork,
    veal or lamb
6 eggs
¼ teaspoon grated nutmeg
300ml/½pint/1¼ cups sunflower oil
8 tablespoons plain white (all-purpose)
    flour
8 tablespoons grated pecorino cheese
6 tablespoons grated dry bread
¼ teaspoon freshly milled black pepper
4 thick slices crusty white bread
125g/4oz/1 cup caciocavallo cheese, or
    very mature Cheddar cheese, coarsely
    grated or cubed
4 or 5 tablespoons freshly grated Parmesan
    cheese

Put the chicken or chickens into the stockpot and cover generously with boiling water. Add the parsley and 1 teaspoon salt. Return to the boil, then simmer for about 2 hours, skimming the surface occasionally with a slotted spoon.

Meanwhile, mix the minced (ground) meat with 2 of the eggs, nutmeg and ¼ teaspoon salt. Shape this mixture into hazelnut-sized meatballs.

Heat the oil until a small piece of bread dropped into it sizzles instantly. Coat the meatballs in about half the flour and fry on all sides until browned, frying in batches if necessary for about 3 minutes. Drain well on kitchen paper (paper towels) and set aside until required.

Next, make the cheese balls. Mix the pecorino and the bread together, then add 2 eggs and the pepper. Make them into tiny balls, about the size of a thumb-nail, and coat them lightly in the remaining flour. Re-heat the oil used to fry the meatballs again and fry the cheese balls until brown and crisp. Drain well on kitchen paper and set aside until required.

When the chicken is cooked to the point where it is almost falling off the bones, take it out of the stockpot and strain the stock. Return the stock to the stockpot and keep it boiling. Pre-heat the grill (broiler) to high.

Beat the remaining 2 eggs and immerse the slices of bread in the egg until soaked through, then grill (broil) them on both sides until toasted and crisp. Cut into small cubes.

Arrange a layer of toasted cubes in the bottom of 4 deep bowls, then add a layer of meatballs and finally a layer of cheese balls. Add a layer of grated or cubed caciocavallo. Pour boiling stock into each bowl, right up to the rim. Finish off with a sprinkling of Parmesan on top of each bowlful. Serve at once.

Tagliolini alla Termolese

Tagliolini with Mussels and Clams

It is sometimes easy to forget that Molise has a coastline of its own, which brings with it a tradition of fish and seafood dishes that one should not ignore. This very simple dish uses fresh mussels and *vongole* in a spicy sauce on freshly prepared tagliolini. You can, of course, use the same sauce with any shape or type of pasta you like.

Serves 4

for the pasta:

400g/14oz/heaped 3 cups plain white (all-purpose) flour

4 eggs

¼ teaspoon salt

for the sauce:

1kg/2lb fresh mussels, cleaned and ready to cook

1kg/2lb fresh clams, cleaned and ready to cook

6 tablespoons olive oil

2 cloves garlic, lightly crushed

1 small dried red chilli pepper

1 large strip fresh red pepper, diced

4 tablespoons dry white wine

salt and freshly milled black pepper

chopped parsley to garnish

Make the pasta first. Pile all the flour on the tabletop and make a hollow in the centre with your fist. Break the eggs into the hollow, add the salt and blend the eggs into the flour, using your fingertips at first, then gradually your whole hand. Knead until you have a smooth mass of dough. Begin to roll out the dough and fold it in half before rolling and folding again as per normal. When you have a sheet of dough which is smooth, translucent and even, dust with flour and roll it up on to itself. Cut it into thin ribbons with a sharp knife and scatter them on to a floured cloth until required. Cover with another floured cloth and make the sauce.

Rinse the shellfish very thoroughly under running water. Discard any that are open, then tip each separately into a large shallow pan. Place them over a medium heat, cover the pans with lids and shake the pans to help all the shells open up. After about 5 minutes, all shells that are going to open will have opened. Discard any that are not open. Take the pans off the heat and leave to stand for a further 2–3 minutes, covered.

Take all the shellfish out of the pans. Strain the liquid from the pans into one bowl and set it to one side. Remove the mussels and clams from the shells and put both in one bowl. Discard the shells. You may like to keep a few of the prettier shells and their contents for garnishing the dish at the end.

Bring a large pan of salted water to a rolling boil. Meanwhile, in a large frying pan (skillet), fry the oil with the garlic, chilli and pepper until the garlic is golden brown and the pepper is soft. Add the shellfish and the wine and heat through for 3–4 minutes, stirring, then add the strained shellfish liquid and continue cooking for a further 3 minutes over a lively heat. Remove from the heat, cover and leave to stand.

Toss the tagliolini into the boiling salted water, stir, return to the boil and cook for about 2 minutes, until tender. Drain well and tip into the pan containing the shellfish. Mix everything together over a very lively heat for about 2 minutes. Scatter with parsley and serve at once.

La Pasta per la Festa

Festival Pasta

Pasta in Molise is much more than something to eat, it is ingrained in the culture as an integral part of the social and economic structure of the region. It is, put simply, part of life.

The reason for the abundance of pasta in this area is due to the huge fields of excellent grain which grow here and the many streams and waterways which were used to power the watermills. These eventually developed into early pasta factories. To the many peasant families and small farmers scattered throughout the region, going into town to buy something which they could make at home seemed completely pointless, and visits into town were extremely rare in any case. The women were used to preparing flour mixed with water to make pasta for the evening meal – the one hot meal their husbands would eat after their day out in the fields. The simple pasta would then have been combined with pork, mushrooms, cheeses, pulses, vegetables, fish, meat or poultry, depending upon the level of poverty of the household or the land surrounding it. The shapes of the pasta would vary from household to household, dependent entirely upon the imagination of the cook!

On High days and Holy days, home-made pasta was, and still is, very much part of the celebrations. It would differ from the plain weekday pasta because eggs would be added to the dough, and the sauce would be richer and more sophisticated. Because factory made durum wheat pasta was such a rarity, as it was only available in the shops in the towns, however, it too was bought and cooked for feast days.

The great Molisan tradition of pasta carries on today. It is a marvellous partnership between tradition, expertise and local custom, even though nowadays most of the grain is imported from the United States and Canada.

Serves 4 to 6

1 onion, chopped
2 cloves garlic, chopped
2 tablespoons chopped fresh parsley
1 very thick slice prosciutto crudo (Parma ham), cubed
4 tablespoons olive oil
1kg/2lb boneless mutton or lamb, such as leg, shoulder or fillet, cubed
5 tablespoons wine
150ml/4 pint/⅔ cup tomato passata
400g/14oz zitoni
salt
8 tablespoons freshly grated Pecorino cheese

Fry the onion, garlic, parsley and prosciutto together in the olive oil in a saucepan until the onion is transparent. Add the meat and brown it all over. Stir in the wine and allow the alcohol to boil off for a few minutes, then pour in the passata and stir thoroughly. Lower the heat to a gentle simmer. Leave to simmer for 2–3 hours, or until the meat is falling apart, stirring occasionally.

Bring a large pan of salted water to a rolling boil. Toss in the pasta, stir, return to the boil and cook until just tender, checking the timing on the pocket. Drain the pasta well.

Arrange 1 layer of pasta on the bottom of a warmed serving dish. Cover with a sprinkling of cheese and a layer of the sauce. Pour the remaining pasta on top, cover with cheese again and the remaining sauce. Mix everything together and cover. Leave to stand for about 3 minutes, then serve.

Conchiglie al Ragù con la Ricotta / Conchiglie with Ragù and Ricotta
(page 69)

Cavatielli al Sugo di Maiale

Cavatielli with Pork Sauce

Cavatielli are the most popular and traditional of all the home-made pasta shapes made in the region. They are fairly similar in texture to the orecchiette of Puglia, although they are made with potatoes and flour and look like elongated seashells. They are made by rubbing sections of dough against the hard, lined surface of a coarse wooden table.

The combination of cavatielli with pork is one of the most characteristic dishes of Molisan cuisine. These days it is prepared at any time of year, for any occasion, although originally it was created in honour of the Feast of Sant'Antonio Abate (Saint Anthony the Abbot) on 17 January. Tradition dictates that on this day, in all the towns and villages throughout the region, but most especially in Campobasso, in front of the church dedicated to the saint, a huge bonfire is lit. The priest stands by the fire and blesses a parade of pigs, who are all decorated with ribbons and bows for the event.

As the day progresses, more and more people come to the fire – each person bringing a piece of wood to add to the fire and keep it going. The old men sit around the edges of the fire and tell stories about 'the old days'. In the evening, everyone heads for home, carrying with them a shovelful of burning embers from the great fire. This is not just to light the way and keep warm, but it is mainly an Act of Devotion to the saint.

Many families slaughter a pig on the eve of 17 January. Once that is done, and the pig is hanging in the cold air, the families invite friends and relations round for the evening for a plate of cavatielli, a game of cards, some wine, olives and bread. In between one glass of wine and the next, they sing the old songs about Saint'Antonio and his epic struggles against the Devil.

Serves 4 to 6

for the pasta:
1kg/2lb floury potatoes
300g/10oz/2¼ cups plain white (all-purpose) flour
pinch of salt
extra flour for dusting

for the sauce:
1 onion, peeled and chopped
2 cloves garlic, chopped
1 dried red chilli pepper
1 thick strip pork belly (belly of pork), cubed
1 big Italian pork sausage, peeled and cubed
1 liver sausage, peeled and cubed, or if unavailable, use another pork sausage
5 tablespoons olive oil
500g/1lb loin of pork, cubed
1.8 litres/3 pints/½ cups tomato passata
salt and freshly milled black pepper

Make the pasta first. Put the potatoes in a large saucepan, cover generously with cold, salted water and bring to the boil. Boil until tender, then drain and peel them quickly while they are still hot. Mash the potatoes finely, using a food mill, letting them fall on to the tabletop in a pile. Add the flour while the potatoes are still warm and knead together thoroughly until you have a smooth, even dough.

Divide the ball of dough in half. Working with 1 ball of dough at a time, roll out the dough on the table to make long ropes about 1cm/½in thick. Cut them into 1cm/½in cubes, then roll them across the tabletop with your fingertips to make elongated, concave shell shapes. Use extra flour for dusting as you work, then arrange all the cavatielli in neat, precise rows on a floured surface. Leave them to dry out until required.

Make the sauce next. Fry the onion, garlic, chilli, pork belly (belly of pork) and sausages with the olive oil for about 15 minutes, stirring frequently, over a gentle heat. Add the pork loin and stir thoroughly. Stir in the passata, then cover and simmer for about 10 minutes. Season to taste, cover again and leave to simmer for 2–2½ hours, or until the meat is completely falling apart.

Bring a large pan of salted water to a rolling boil. Put half the sauce at the bottom of a warmed serving bowl and keep it hot. When the water boils, slide in the cavatielli and stir them carefully so as not to break them. Return to the boil. As soon as the cavatielli bob back to the surface, scoop them out with a slotted spoon, shake off any excess water and tip them into the bowl with the sauce. Continue in this way until all have been cooked. Stir the sauce and the cavatielli together gently, gradually adding the remaining sauce as you stir. Serve at once.

Conchiglie al Ragù con la Ricotta

Pasta with Ragù and Ricotta

This is one of those magical, relatively quick dishes that tastes as though it has taken hours of dedicated work! You must use best-quality Italian sausages and really fresh ricotta for the best results.

Serves 4

3–4 tablespoons fruity olive oil
½ onion, sliced 'like a veil'
1 thick slice very fatty prosciutto crudo (Parma ham), cubed
200g/7oz Italian sausages, peeled and crumbled
150ml/5fl oz dry red or white wine
500ml/¾ pint/2 cups tomato passata
salt and freshly milled black pepper
400g/14oz *conchiglie* shaped pasta
250g/8oz/1 cup fresh ricotta cheese
50g/2oz/½ cup freshly grated pecorino cheese

Fry together the oil, onion and prosciutto very gently for about 5 minutes. Add the sausage meat and mix together very thoroughly. Stir in the wine and allow the wine to evaporate for about 2 minutes, then stir in the passata. Cover and leave to simmer for about 50 minutes, stirring occasionally.

Bring a large pan of salted water to a rolling boil. Toss in the conchiglie, stir, return to the boil and cook the pasta until just tender, checking the packet for exact timing.

Meanwhile, mash the ricotta with 2–3 tablespoons of the ragù to make it more manageable. Drain the pasta and return it to the pan, add the sauce and the ricotta and mix it all together. Transfer into a warmed serving bowl. Scatter with the pecorino and serve at once.

Spaghetti con le Anguille
Spaghetti with Eels

This is a typical Christmas Eve dish, when meat eating is out of the question among the more fervently religious families. In many households which still respect the old traditions, the Christmas Eve feast cannot begin until the head of the household, standing next to the fireplace, has blessed the big, slow-burning stump that was saved for this purpose. Next to him stands the woman of the house, holding the grill used to cook a gigantic Christmas Eve eel. This is a night of magic, when the old grannies whisper to their granddaughters the words of the spells which will remove the evil eye, and the glowing stump in the grate becomes the guest of honour. No morsel of food can be eaten without first offering some to the burning tree stump: it represents light and life.

So, at the end of each year, with the burning wood representing the renewal of life itself, and the start of a new beginning, the ashes from the burned stump are thrown out on to the soil. This represents the end of a year's misery and hardship, while at the same time preparing the ground for a better harvest next year. Each glass of wine raised to the burning stump is representative of the blood of Christ, which will purify the soul of all those who drink it. This paganistic/religious ceremony is carried out with great solemnity by all those who really believe in the magic of Christmas Eve. Only in this way will tempest, disease and misfortune be kept at bay throughout the next year! The recipe which follows developed out of the original simple dish of grilled eel.

Serves 4

800g/1¾lb fresh eels, gutted and cleaned
coarse sea salt
bran
1 onion, peeled and sliced
5 tablespoons olive oil
2 tablespoons chopped fresh parsley
1 dried red chilli pepper
1.2 litres/2 pints/5 cups tomato passata
400g/14oz spaghetti

Rub the eels firmly all over with handfuls of coarse salt and bran. This removes all the hard skins and scales, and is an operation which used to be carried out with handfuls of rough ash from the tree stump (see intro).

Wash the skinned fish very thoroughly in running water. Cut off the fins with scissors. Slit open the fish and gut them carefully, removing the heads. Slice all the fish into 6cm/2½in chunks. Set aside.

Fry the onion in the olive oil until soft, then add the parsley and the chilli. Cook for about 5 minutes, then add the passata, a pinch of salt and the eels. Cover and simmer gently, shaking the pan occasionally but not stirring, for about 20 minutes, or until the fish are cooked through and the flesh flakes easily.

Bring a large saucepan of salted water to a rolling boil. Toss in the spaghetti, stir, return to the boil and cook until the spaghetti is just tender. Drain well and return to the saucepan. Pour over the eel sauce and mix together thoroughly. Transfer to a platter and serve at once.

Tacchino Ripieno alla Molisana

Stuffed Roast Turkey

The white fleshed, super lean turkey which now lines the supermarket shelves all over the world is a far cry from the locally bred *vicce*, which until very recently was considered to be a bird of such luxury and value in Molise. It was reared on local farms in very small numbers for Christmas and New Year, when it would be presented with much pomp and circumstance to the *signori* of the village: the priest, the doctor, the chemist, the mayor, the lawyer and so on.

Naturally, to be absolutely certain that the bird was fresh and genuine, it would be delivered alive, tied by the feet and held upside down. Many of the birds understandably reacted very strongly to this treatment, and in some houses the 'gift' would lead to so much fear and apprehension that it would be passed on to someone else. There has been more than one occasion where the bird has been handed around so often that it has eventually ended up back with the original donor! The very best *vicce*, or so they say locally, is one fed on hot bran mash and mountain grown wheat.

Serves 8

one 5kg/10lb oven-ready turkey, with
    turkey giblets reserved
8 tablespoons olive oil
½ onion, peeled and chopped
salt and freshly milled black pepper
125g/4oz/2 cups fresh white breadcrumbs
2 eggs, beaten
3 tablespoons freshly grated pecorino
    cheese
2 tablespoons pine kernels
2 tablespoons dried currants, soaked in
    warm water for 15 minutes, then
    thoroughly drained
2 tablespoons chopped fresh parsley
¼ teaspoon grated nutmeg
2 cloves garlic, crushed
1 tablespoon fresh rosemary leaves, finely
    chopped
1 tablespoon whole black peppercorns
3 fresh sage leaves
5 tablespoons dry white wine

Pre-heat the oven to 180°C/350°F/Gas Mark 4. Wash and dry the turkey inside and out carefully. Trim the giblets and put them into a saucepan with 1 tablespoon of olive oil and the onion. Fry gently until the onion is soft and the giblets are browned. Put them into a bowl, and leave to cool. When cool, thoroughly mix in the breadcrumbs, eggs, cheese, pine kernels, currants, parsley and nutmeg. Season to taste with salt and freshly milled black pepper.

Add 1 tablespoon of olive oil, mix again and then use this mixture to stuff the turkey. Secure it closed tightly.

Grease a roasting pan with half the remaining oil. Chop the garlic and rosemary together finely, then mix into the remaining oil. Stir in the peppercorns and add salt to taste. Chop the sage leaves and mix them into the oil. Add the wine and then use this mixture to brush all over the turkey, keeping half to baste the bird as it roasts.

Roast the turkey for about 3½ hours, basting frequently, until the juices run clear when the thickest part of the thigh is pierced and the skin is golden brown and crisp. Leave to rest for at least 15 minutes, then carve and serve.

Gallina Ripiena in Brodo
Stuffed Boiled Chicken

Serving broth as a first course, either with pasta or rice cooked in it or not, is very much a feature throughout the region of the more refined and elegant dinners prepared in honour of special occasions such as Christmas and Easter. The chicken, with its delicious stuffing, appears among the two or three main course dishes, *after* the pasta which follows the soup!

With the chicken, according to the best Molisan tradition, you will normally find tiny little fried meatballs, stewed greens, such as escarole, fried croûtons and dishes of *pasta reale*. The most unusual side dish, however, consists of small bowls of sour cherry jam, which gives this dish a unique sweet-and-sour quality.

Serves 4

1.2kg/4lb free-range chicken, with giblets
2 tablespoons olive oil
salt and freshly milled black pepper
1 onion, peeled
1 stick celery, washed
1 carrot, scraped and quartered
2–3 sprigs fresh parsley

for the stuffing:
4 tablespoons fresh white breadcrumbs
1 egg, beaten
3 tablespoons freshly grated pecorino
   cheese
2 cloves garlic, chopped
3 tablespoons chopped fresh parsley
¼ teaspoon freshly grated nutmeg
¼ teaspoon freshly milled black pepper

Rinse and pat dry the chicken very thoroughly inside and out. Rinse the giblets and chop them finely. Fry the giblets in the olive oil for just a few minutes, or until sealed and brown all over. Season thoroughly with salt and pepper and take off the heat. Mix the cooked giblets with all the other stuffing ingredients and moisten with a little water if necessary. Use this stuffing to fill the chicken and sew it closed with cooks string.

Bring a pan of salted water to the boil with the onion, celery, carrot and parsley. Immerse the stuffed chicken, and simmer for 1½ hours, or until the chicken is cooked through and the juices run clear if the thickest part of the thigh is pierced.

Remove the meat from the broth and carve. Arrange each portion on a warmed plate with a little stuffing and some sour cherry jam to serve.

Sciurille

Fried Courgette Flowers

The beauty about growing your own courgettes (or zucchini, as you might prefer to call them) is that as long as you look after them fairly carefully, they are quite easy to handle. Especially as they have a knack of always producing masses of their orange flowers, even if they do not provide you with many vegetables! The flowers taste truly delicious, provided you remove the inner pistil from each one and allow them to soak in very cold water for about an hour before drying and using. These two simple procedures remove every trace of bitterness from the flowers.

Serves 4

500g/1lb courgette (zucchini) flowers, pistils removed and soaked in cold water
150g/5oz mozzarella
4 canned anchovy fillets rinsed, dried and chopped
4 tablespoons plain white (all-purpose) flour
3 eggs
1 litre/1¾ pints/4½ cups sunflower oil
salt

Drain the flowers very carefully by lightly shaking off all the water. Dry each one as much as possible with kitchen towel (paper towels).

Push a small piece of mozzarella and a little chopped anchovy inside each flower and fold the petals over to conceal the filling. Cover each flower lightly in flour and then immerse in the beaten egg.

Heat the oil until a small piece of bread dropped into the oil sizzles instantly. Fry the egg-coated flowers in batches until crisp and golden brown on both sides. Drain well on kitchen paper, sprinkle lightly with salt and serve at once.

Frittelle di Fiore di Sambuco

Elderflower Fritters

Another recipe which uses as its main ingredient something which is completely free and can be picked in the hedgerows in June when the elderflower bushes are in bloom.

Serves 4

8 sprigs fresh elderflowers
2 eggs
2 tablespoons plain white (all-purpose) flour
¼ teaspoon salt
sunflower oil for deep-frying

Rinse the elderflowers and pat them dry. Beat the eggs, gradually adding the flour in a steady stream to prevent lumps forming. Season with the salt and dilute with enough cold water to make a batter which has the same consistency of thick yogurt. Immerse the elderflowers in the batter.

Heat the oil until a small piece of bread dropped into the oil sizzles instantly. Take the flowers out of the oil and fry them until they become puffy and golden brown, about 3 or 4 minutes. Remove them from the oil with a slotted spoon, drain on kitchen paper (paper towels) and serve at once.

Cime di Ortica Stufate

Stewed Nettles

The custom of cooking nettles comes from the simple reason that they grow in such profusion along the pathways, so even the poorest and most humble peasant could enjoy a green vegetable. Originally, the tradition of cooking nettles came from next door Puglia, brought into Molise by the shepherds on their way through the region. The tradition of the Transumanza brought many new and different ideas into the region.

Serves 4

1kg/2lb fresh nettle tops
4 tablespoons olive oil
1 onion, peeled and thinly sliced
salt and freshly milled black pepper

Wash and prepare the nettle tops, selecting only the youngest and most tender shoots. Dry them in a cloth and set aside.

Heat the oil in a deep frying pan (skillet) and fry the onion until soft. Add the nettles and season with salt and pepper. Stir together, cover and simmer slowly for about 30 minutes or until soft, adding a little hot water occasionally if necessary. Serve at once.

Insalata di Dente di Leone

Dandelion Leaf Salad

The more common name for this humble garden weed, a very close relative of chicory (Belgian endive), is *piscialetto*. The word means 'wet the bed' in literal translation, which ought to tell you something about the diuretic qualities of the dandelion! You must pick the dandelion for this salad just after the very first winter frosts. Dig deep into the ground to expose as much of the roots as you can; they will be pure white at this time of year. Extract the entire plant, and rinse it very thoroughly before using. As this salad has a somewhat bitter taste, it is wise to think carefully about what you serve with it.

Serves 4 to 6

1kg/2lb dandelion plants (not the
    flowers), well rinsed and dried
olive oil
salt and freshly milled black pepper

Slice the dandelion leaves and roots very finely. Transfer to a salad bowl. Dress to taste with olive oil and salt and pepper. Serve.

Riso e Verza

Rice and Green Cabbage

Some readers might question the presence of rice in this almost entirely pasta based cuisine. Yet, this is not a Lombard dish which has slipped southwards, nor a North African/Arabic eating habit which has crept north via Sicily. The fact is, that in the last century, in the Trigno valley, there were some rice

*Insalata di Dente di Leone/Dandelion Leaf Salad, and Verza
e Fagioli/Savoy Cabbage and Beans (page 77)*

fields. The town of Mafalda, before taking on this marvellous name, was called Ripalta sul Riso.

Although these paddy fields were not very big, you have to take into account that the local eating custom was to consume all that was produced locally, without exporting it outside the region and without importing very much in. So rice would have found its way quite naturally into the local gastronomy, even among the lowliest of peasant families. Recipes using rice which are peculiar only to this one area came into use and are still in use here today: long after the rice fields have gone.

Serves 4

1 Savoy cabbage, coarsely shredded
150ml/5fl oz/⅔ cup olive oil
1 large onion, peeled and chopped
2 canned tomatoes, drained, seeded and finely chopped
200g/7oz/1 cup arborio or nano fino rice
salt
5 tablespoons grated pecorino or Parmesan cheese

Fry the cabbage, oil, onion and tomatoes together in a very large saucepan for a few minutes, stirring constantly. Add a little boiling water and cook the cabbage about 6 minutes, stirring frequently and gradually adding more water.

When the cabbage is soft and the water is covering it, stir in the rice and slowly cook the rice, for about 15 minutes, adding more boiling water as required. Season to taste and simmer until the rice is very soft. Transfer to a serving bowl and sprinkle with the cheese. Serve at once.

Terrina di Patate, Cipolle e Pomodoro

Potato, Onion and Tomato Bake

A delicious and very easy layered dish using the humble potato and onion, plus a little tomato for colour and freshness of flavour. This is an ideal light lunch dish, served with a big green salad and some crusty, warm garlic bread.

Serves 4

4 large potatoes, peeled
salt and freshly milled black pepper
1½ tablespoons dried oregano
9 tablespoons olive oil
4 tablespoons fresh white breadcrumbs
3 red onions, peeled and sliced into thin rings
3 very large, ripe beefsteak or marmande tomatoes, sliced

Cover the potatoes with cold water and boil for 4 minutes, then drain and slice into thin discs. Grease a ovenproof dish large enough to take all the vegetables and begin to arrange in layers. Start with potatoes: sprinkle with salt and pepper, oregano, a little oil and a few pinches of breadcrumbs. Cover with tomatoes and onions and repeat. Continue in this way until all the ingredients have been used up. Finish off with a layer of tomatoes covered in oil, oregano, salt and pepper and a generous coating of breadcrumbs. Leave to stand for a few minutes while you pre heat the oven to 180°C/350°F/Gas Mark 4.

Bake for about 30 minutes, or until the top is browned and crisp. Serve warm.

Caponata
Bread, Egg and Tomato Salad

This is Molise's version of a dish which appears all over southern Italy, in various guises: from the incredibly over-the-top Baroque Sicilian version, which has deep-fried aubergines (egg plants), celery and octopus making up the salad and a chocolate and almond coating, to the spartan bread and tomato salad of Basilicata.

This recipe evolved in the *cantine* of Molise, which the local men have always used as a meeting place for playing cards, discussing politics, gossiping and sometimes having a bite to eat. This dish is designed to encourage drinking rather than to fill the stomach! Ideally, this dish requires hard, plain, savoury biscuits called *taralli* to give the dish true authenticity, but thinly sliced stale white Italian bread, such as ciabatta, makes a perfectly adequate substitute.

Serves 4

4 *taralli*, or 4 slices stale white bread, such
    as ciabatta or casareccio
1½ tablespoons white wine vinegar
4 firm, ripe tomatoes, rinsed and sliced
1 cucumber, peeled and sliced
1 large juicy pepper, seeded, cored and sliced
8 black (ripe) olives
8 green olives
2 cloves garlic, sliced
2 sticks celery, sliced
3 hard-boiled eggs, shelled and sliced
125g/4oz canned anchovies, drained
1 heaped teaspoon dried oregano
125ml/4fl oz/½ cup olive oil
salt and freshly milled black pepper, or
    finely crushed chillies

Lay the *taralli* or the bread on a clean napkin. Sprinkle thoroughly with the vinegar, then wrap in the napkin and leave to stand for about 10 minutes. Take them out of the napkin and arrange on a serving dish.

Arrange the tomatoes and cucumber slices on top. Put the slices of pepper on top and then insert olives and slivers of garlic here and there in the pile. Scatter over the celery, then add the hard-boiled eggs and the anchovies. Sprinkle generously with oregano.

Pour over the olive oil to thoroughly cover the salad. Season with salt and pepper, or the crushed chillis, and chill in the refrigerator for 30 minutes before serving.

Verza e Fagioli
Savoy Cabbage with Beans

This is that sort of very basic, simple peasant dish which can be varied almost endlessly thanks to the substitution or addition of a handful of rice, a little pasta, lentils instead of beans, and so on. A classic winter warmer, this is delicious with plenty of olive oil soaked, hot ciabatta bread.

Serves 4

300g/10oz/1⅔ cup dried borlotti beans
1 Savoy cabbage
6 tablespoons olive oil
2 cloves garlic, peeled
1 small dried red chilli
salt

Soak the beans overnight in cold water. Rinse and put in a saucepan. Cover with fresh water and bring to a rolling boil and boil for about 5 minutes. Drain and rinse under cold running water. Return to the saucepan and cover with fresh water. Slowly bring to the boil, then simmer gently until completely soft. Only add salt to the beans once they have become really soft otherwise the salt will toughen the skins.

Meanwhile, tear the cabbage apart and rinse all the leaves. Discard any leaves that are too tough and discard the core and all tough spines. Cut the cabbage into rough pieces and rinse and dry it again. Boil it in salted water until soft, then set aside without draining it.

When the beans are soft, heat the oil and fry the garlic and chilli in another large saucepan until the garlic is golden brown. Add the beans and cabbage alternately with their water, stirring together as you combine all the ingredients. Finally add salt to taste. Cover and simmer for 10–15 minutes (or longer) before serving.

Bum

Jam and Custard Tart

This delicious dessert with the very strange name is actually a very simple *crostata*, a tart with a criss-cross lattice decoration on the top and a filling of lemon custard and sour cherry jam. Try as I might, I have been unable to discover why it is called *BUM*, but this is its only authentic name in the region, and all I can say is that it tastes delicious!

Serves 8

butter for greasing pan

for the pastry:
500g/1lb/4 cups plain white (all-purpose) flour
250g/8oz/heaped 1 cup granulated sugar
250g/8oz/1 cup lard, diced
4 egg yolks
1 egg

for the filling:
4 egg yolks
8 tablespoons caster (superfine) sugar
8 tablespoons plain white (all-purpose) flour
1 litre/1¾ pints/4½ cups milk, warm
grated rind (peel) of 1 lemon
9 tablespoons sour cherry jam

Butter a 27.5cm/11in tart pan with a removable bottom.

Make the pastry (dough) first. Pile all the flour on the worktop and make a hollow in the centre with your fist. Add the sugar and the lard, then add the egg yolks and the whole egg, kneading together with your hands to make a smooth dough. Cover with a cloth and leave it to rest for about 30 minutes.

Now make the filling. Beat the egg yolks, together in a heatproof bowl with the sugar until pale and fluffy. Beat in the flour, then gradually beat in the milk. Place the bowl over a pan of boiling water and beat the custard with the balloon whisk until thick enough to coat the back of a metal spoon. Stir in the lemon rind (peel), then set aside to cool slightly.

Pre-heat the oven to 190°C/375°F/Gas Mark 5. Roll out about three-quarters of the pastry and line the tart tin, reserving the remaining pastry to make a lattice on the top. Pour the custard into the tart case and dot all over with the jam. Roll out the remaining pastry, cut it into strips about 30cm/12in and lay over the tart to make a lattice pattern, cutting off the overhang. Bake for about 1 hour, or until golden brown and set. Serve this dish either hot or cold.

Castagnelle
Chocolate-covered Biscuits

This recipe is an adaptation from the original hundred-year-old recipe as prepared in the beautiful mountain town of Agnone. The original recipe calls for the use of a local cooking pot called a *tiella*, made of copper with two handles and a lid.

To bake these biscuits (cookies), traditionally a few raw *castagnelle* are laid inside the pot, which is then buried in hot embers and ash in the fire. Baked in this way, they apparently acquire a unique flavour and texture. Agnone is famous for its twin industries, copper and sweet making, and for being a cultural centre in the region.

Makes about 30 biscuits (cookies)

750g/1½lb/5½ cups plain white (all-purpose) flour
10 eggs
3 tablespoons sugar
3 tablespoons olive oil
1 teaspoon vanilla essence (extract)
extra oil for greasing
extra flour for dusting

for the icing (frosting):
1kg/2lb/5 cups sugar
500g/1lb couverture chocolate, broken into small pieces
1 tablespoon cocoa powder

Pre-heat the oven to 200°C/400°F/Gas Mark 6. Place all the flour in a pile on the tabletop, make a hollow in the centre with your fist. Break the eggs into the hollow. Add the sugar, oil and vanilla. Beat them into the flour using a fork, then knead with your hands. Form the dough into a ball, then roll it out into thumb-thick cylinders. Cut into 5cm/2in strips and lay them side by side on oiled and flour dusted baking sheets.

Bake for about 10 minutes, until they split open slightly 'so their soul can fly out' and the biscuits go quite brown. The main thing is that they must be dry and crisp.

Meanwhile, prepare the icing (frosting). Put 6 tablespoons cold water and the sugar into a large saucepan over a very low heat and melt the sugar into a thick, clear syrup. When the sugar is thick enough to form a ball when dropped into water, add the chocolate and the cocoa. Stir constantly until the chocolate melts and the icing is smooth.

Remove the icing from the heat and quickly dip each biscuit (cookie) into the chocolate, holding them on the end of a fork. Leave them to dry out on a wire rack until the chocolate is set, then serve. Remember that to be authentic, they need to have a really thick chocolate coating, thick enough for your teeth to bury themselves in it!!

'Cauciune' di Natale

Christmas Pastries

This Christmas Eve speciality is typical of one of those ancient recipes whose origins are lost in historical rituals and hard work. To test if the oil for frying the pastries is hot enough, it is traditional to drop a small piece of pastry in and watch it sizzle while silently making a wish for the coming year.

Makes about 20

sunflower oil for deep-frying
3 tablespoons icing (confectioners') sugar
1 heaped teaspoon ground cinnamon

for the filling:
500g/1lb/2¼ cups dried chick-peas
3 tablespoons unsweetened cocoa powder
3 tablespoons caster (superfine) sugar
200g/7oz crystallized (candied) citrus
    peel, chopped
3 tablespoons very liquid honey
2 tablespoons sweet liquer of your choice

for the pastry:
500g/1lb/4 cups plain white (all-purpose)
    flour, sifted
6 tablespoons olive oil

¼ teaspoon salt
2 teaspoons vanilla essence (extract)
4 tablespoons dry white wine

Cover the chick-peas in cold water and leave them to soak overnight, preferably out of doors on a frosty night.

The next day, drain and rinse the chick-peas, then put in a pan and cover with fresh water. Boil for 5 minutes, drain and rinse them again. Cover with fresh water and simmer for about 3 hours, or until completely tender and almost pulpy. Drain and push them through a food mill or a sieve (strainer) to make a purée.

Mix the chick-pea purée with the cocoa powder, sugar, citrus peel, honey and liquer to make a smooth filling. Set aside until required to allow the flavours to develop.

Now make the pastry (dough). Pile all the flour on the worktop and make a hollow in the centre with your fist. Put the oil, salt, vanilla essence (extract) and half the wine into the hole and knead until you have a very smooth, shiny and elastic dough, adding more wine as necessary.

Roll out the dough as thinly as possible. Cut it into 7cm/3in circles with a pastry cutter. Put a spoonful of filling on one half of each circle, then fold the circles in half and press them closed using the prongs of a fork.

Heat the oil in a deep-fat fryer until a small piece of pastry dropped into it sizzles and goes golden almost immediately (don't forget to make a wish!) Fry the *cauciuni*, 4 or 5 at a time depending upon the size of your deep-fat fryer. As soon as the *cauciuni* are puffy and golden brown, take them out of the hot oil with a slotted spoon and drain them on kitchen paper (paper towels), keeping them warm. Continue until all have been fried, then dust them generously with icing (confectioners') sugar and cinnamon. Serve piping hot.

Biscotti Ripieni

Stuffed Biscuits

These biscuits (cookies) have a deliciously rich almond and grape jelly filling.

Makes about 30

for the filling:
750g/1½lb grape jelly
250g/8oz blanched almonds, finely ground
2 tablespoons fresh white breadcrumbs
3 tablespoons couverture chocolate, chopped
2 tablespoons sweet dessert wine

for the biscuits (cookies):
1.3kg/3lb plain white (all-purpose) flour
500ml/¾pint/2 cups milk
250ml/8fl oz/1 cup olive oil
5 eggs
500g/1lb/2½ cups caster (superfine) sugar
grated rind (peel) of 2 lemons
1 heaped teaspoon cream of tartare
2 egg yolks, beaten with 2 tablespoons icing (confectioners') sugar
butter for greasing
extra flour for dusting

Make the filling first. Mix the jelly and the ground almonds together. Stir in the breadcrumbs, chocolate and the wine. Set aside until required.

Pre-heat the oven to 190°C/375°F/Gas Mark 5.

Now make the pastry (dough). Pile all the flour on the worktop and make a hollow in the centre with your fist. Mix the milk, oil, eggs, sugar, lemon rind (peel) and cream of tartare together very thoroughly. Blend into the flour, using your hands to knead until you have an elastic dough which you can roll out.

Roll out the dough and cut out various shapes of roughly the same size with a pastry wheel, making them large enough to be filled and folded in half. You can make whatever shapes take your fancy, as long as they are all large enough to have some of the filling inside. Fold over and seal closed with great care so none of the filling can escape during baking. Butter and flour some baking sheets and lay the filled biscuits (cookies) on them.

Brush the biscuits with the egg yolk and icing (confectioners') sugar mixture. Bake for about 15 minutes, or until they are golden brown and crisp. Cool on wire racks and serve just warm or cold. Store in an air-tight container.

Campania

Campania

The cuisine of Naples and of Campania is so sunny and so full of imagination that it has inspired the local poets and songwriters to exalt and describe its virtues to the point where they have now become a part of Italy's literary world as well as an integral part of the country's gastronomy.

'From the earliest hours of the morning a delicate vapour forms over the terracotta pots in which onion turns golden and basil, freshly plucked from the window box, gives off its noble essence' (from *The Gold of Naples by Marotta*). This is just a sample of the kind of prose which has been written about the food of this region. It is about the much-loved tomato sauce that is such an essential part of the local menu, served on pasta, naturally! For a basic meat and tomato sauce (called ragù) to be acceptable to the local cooks in Campania, it must never be left alone while it cooks, because 'a ragù left alone stops being a ragù and even loses any possibility of becoming one' (anon). To hear one of these cooks describe how to make a simple sauce to pour over pasta is much more like listening to the explanation of a complicated scientific experiment, for these two elements seem to be taken more seriously here than anywhere else. Incidentally, the sauce should 'pulse through maccheroni like blood in a vein' (anon).

Considering the Campanian passion for the tomato, and the extent to which it is used in local dishes, one wonders how they ever managed without it! It was mentioned in a popular Neapolitan song as early as 1743, but was only really used in the kitchen from the end of the eighteenth century and beginning of the nineteenth. It is without question the most important symbol of the local cuisine. In fact, they go so far as to call it a 'half religion'.

As the popularity of the tomato took hold, a canning industry grew up in the region, which has since brought canned tomatoes and tomato paste to the rest of the world.

Pizza is probably the most famous of all the Neapolitan culinary creations, and one of the oldest. It dates much farther back than the use of the tomato. In fact the Ancient Romans used to make a kind of pizza that was simply smeared with olive oil and seasoned with salt – very much like focaccia. It later evolved to the point where it was flavoured with crumbled bay leaves and smeared with lard. The pizza as we know it now, covered with tomatoes and herbs, is a little over two hundred years old. It became extremely popular very quickly, not only with the commoners, but also with the barons and princes of the Court. The Bourbons were particularly partial to pizza, and Ferdinand IV used the ovens at Capodimonte, the same ovens used to bake the famous porcelain, for his pizza. In 1889, the most famous pizza maker of them all, Raffaelle Esposito, created the tricolour Pizza Margherita in honour of the visit to Naples from Piedmont of Queen Margherita di Savoia. There is no limit to the range of pizza toppings, other than the extent of the cook's imagination, but they always have tomatoes – at least in Naples and Campania they do!

Although pasta was not actually invented in Naples, the people of this region have taken it very much to their hearts and over the years have perfected methods of drying and storing it, which began in the little town of Gragnano. This led to the birth of another very successful local industry, the production of dried durum wheat pasta of excellent quality. The variety of shapes and sizes available locally is unrivalled anywhere else in the country.

Milk products are very important in the cuisine of Campania. Provolone, ricotta, scamorza and caciocavallo all frequently appear on the table throughout the region, but the king of all the locally made cheeses has to be mozzarella. The production of this fresh, sweet, tender, spun cheese, the best variety of which is made with buffalo milk, is concentrated in the areas of Aversa, Battipaglia, Capula, Eboli, Aurunca and Sessa. To eat freshly made mozzarella in any of these areas is a gastronomic experience which is very hard to forget! One of the most interesting varieties of mozzarella is called 'burrielli' and consists of bite-sized, very sweet mozzarella which is placed inside terracotta jars and covered with milk. Unfortunately, real buffalo milk mozzarella is becoming very rare, and one often has to put up with the less flavoursome, cow's milk variety, which should properly be called fiordilatte.

In the Neapolitan gastronomic tradition, there is a whole range of dishes that come from the French school of cooking, which was in favour with many of the noble families of Naples, particularly during the last centuries. Recipes thus evolved in which French styles of cookery and ingredients were mixed with those of Naples. In the households where cooks were employed to create such dishes, the entire planning and preparation was left up to them. The cooks would take on the name of the household in order to be easily identified. The results are elaborate and spectacular, like Timballo di Maccheroni.

Such dishes were far beyond the means of the populace, who continued to thrive quite happily on the more simple foods which formed their daily diet. These are still very much in existence today, the obvious example being pasta with tomato sauce, which has been the most important everyday dish of this region ever since its creation. Other specialities include the superb Fritto Misto, simply cooked chicken casseroles and meat dishes, fresh salads and other vegetable dishes.

Not to be forgotten is the imaginative range of traditional pastries such as the ubiquitous babà, delicious taralli, sweet calzoni, fruit flans, sfogliatelle, spumoni and the magnificent pastiera, the delicately flavoured pie filled with rice or swollen wheat grain mixed with ricotta, candied peel and flavoured traditionally with orange blossom water. Campania celebrates her love of good food with a sweet toothed flourish.

Sea food plays an important part in the cuisine of Campania. The fish dishes of Campania tend to use cod, clams and other shellfish, often cooked with tomatoes and herbs, always with flair and imagination.

Most of Campania's 'places of interest' are easy to reach from Naples itself. Among the most memorable and interesting is the ancient city of Paestum. It lies south of Naples, in the rather desolate area of marshland at the southern end of the bay of Salerno. This is one of the most important archaeological sites in the world, and is not to be missed, particularly in the late afternoon or early evening, when the three 2,600-year-old temples turn pink as the sun begins to set.

There is an extraordinary dignity and solemnity about this spellbinding place. The city, founded by the pleasure-loving Sybarites around 700 BC, was once famous for its extremely profitable perfume industry, and glorious roses and violets used to proliferate here. It was originally called Poseidonia, in honour of Poseidon, the god of the sea. Long before the Saracens came to ravage this area, and the malarial marshes took their toll on the population, Paestum's three temples, Hera I, Hera II and the temple of Athena, were turned into churches. In the eighth century AD, the remaining inhabitants of the ancient city settled in the hills at Capaccio Vecchio. Here they built a church called the Madonna of the Pomegranate, thus linking the Christian and Ancient Greek religions, for the pomegranate was the fertility symbol of the goddess Hera. The annual ceremony of carrying flowers in little boats to the church is performed today just as it was in Paestum thousands of years ago, when the flower girls would carry their floral tributes to Hera. In the museum, you can see the evidence of these ancient rituals. Small terracotta figurines hold boats filled with flowers, and the statuettes of Hera show her holding a baby and a pomegranate. Nearby is the gallery which contains the wall paintings from the ancient cemetery found near the city. Of these, the most famous and remarkable is the picture of the diver. These paintings, dating from the fifth century BC, are thought to be the oldest surviving examples of Greek wall painting.

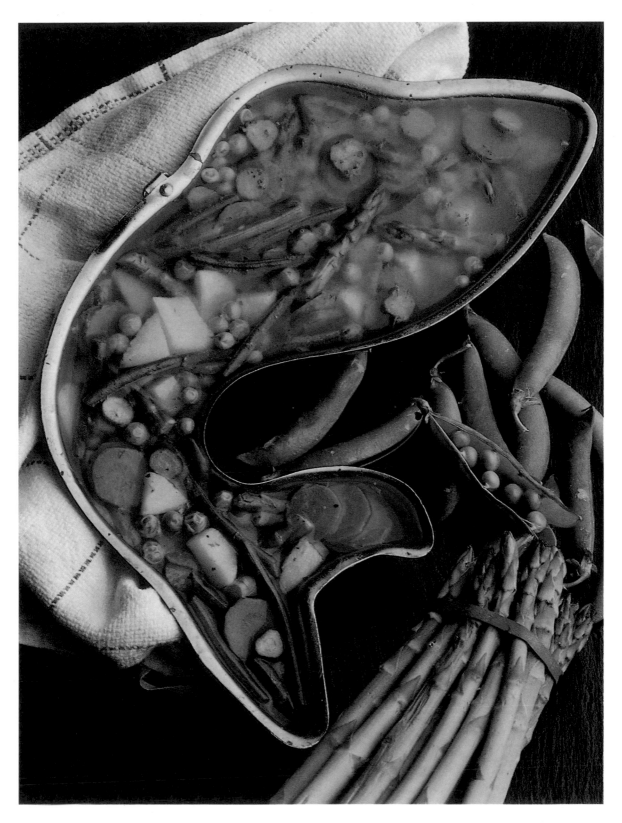

Paté Freddo di Ortaggi/Cold Vegetable Pâté (page 88)

Paté Freddo di Ortaggi

Cold Vegetable Pâté

A classical aspic-style dish made with gelatine dissolved in vegetable stock. This is not what you would normally associate with the cuisine of southern Italy, but it is a Neapolitan recipe which obviously has very strong Parisian origins. It is a very pretty summer dish.

Serves 4

300g/10oz potatoes, peeled
300g/10oz carrots, scraped
125g/4oz asparagus spears
150g/5oz runner beans, topped and tailed
200g/7oz shelled peas, or frozen *petit pois*
1 heaped teaspoon French mustard
juice of ½ lemon
50g/2oz pickled gerkins, chopped
2 teaspoons chopped fresh parsley
salt and freshly milled black pepper
600ml/1 pint/2½ cups vegetable stock
1½ teaspoons powdered gelatine
3 tablespoons Marsala or dry sherry
freshly made mayonnaise, to serve

to garnish:
fresh parsley sprigs
lemon wedges
sliced carrots

Boil or steam the potatoes and carrots separately until tender. Drain and dice them and set aside. Boil or steam all the remaining vegetables separately, then drain them and leave to cool.

When all the vegetables are cold, mix them together gently. Mix the mustard and the lemon juice together, then stir in the gerkins and the parsley. Pour this mixture over the vegetables and stir all gently together. Season with salt and freshly milled black pepper and leave to stand.

Bring the stock to the boil, take off the heat and sprinkle over the gelatine, whisking constantly. When all the gelatine has dissolved, stir in the Marsala, then pour about 2.5cm/1in of the aspic into 2.4 litre/4 pint/10 cup ring mould. Leave to cool and set completely. When the aspic has set, tip in all the vegetables and press them down flat quite firmly with the back of a spoon. Pour more aspic over the vegetables to come up to about 7.5cm/3in from the mould's rim.

Leave to stand until cool, then refrigerate until completely set. Leave remaining aspic to set in a separate container.

Ten minutes or so before serving, dip the mould in boiling hot water for a few seconds, then turn out on to a serving platter. Finely dice the remaining aspic and use to garnish the mould. Decorate with the remaining solid aspic, parsley, lemon wedges and the carrots. Serve immediately with a sauce boat filled with freshly made mayonnaise.

Maccheroni ai Sette Odori

Maccheroni with Seven Flavours

This is the most famous pasta dish of the lovely village of Positano. Few things are more inspiring and beautiful than the views from the top of the cliff at Positano, or the incredible winding road which takes you out of the squalor and chaos of Naples into the bright sunlight and greenery of the coastline. In Positano, the pace of life slows down, and time is dedicated to the enjoyment of the scenery and the blue sea. The sauce is best if made the day before, although you can make it about two hours in advance. You must have really ripe, soft fresh tomatoes for this dish.

If the fact that this recipe is called *maccheroni*, even though the pasta used is actually spaghetti, confuses you, do not despair! In Campania, especially among the 'old boys', *maccheroni* is a generic term for all pasta!

Serves 4

600g/1¼lb fresh, ripe tomatoes
1 clove garlic, crushed
3 tablespoons olive oil
10 leaves fresh basil, torn into small shreds
2 tablespoons chopped fresh parsley
1 teaspoon dried oregano
½ onion, peeled and chopped very finely
1 stick celery, very finely chopped
salt and freshly milled black pepper
400g/14oz spaghetti

Put the tomatoes into a large heatproof bowl and pour boiling water over them to cover. Leave until the skins burst, then drain well. Peel them carefully, then cut them in half and remove the seeds. Quarter and place in a colander, set over a bowl, to drain for 30 minutes.

When the tomatoes are drained, tip them into the bowl. Add the garlic, olive oil, basil, parsley, oregano, onion and celery. These are the seven flavours and must be carefully stirred into the tomatoes. Season with salt and freshly milled black pepper and leave this mixture to stand overnight or for at least 2 hours.

When you are ready to serve, bring a large pan of salted water to a rolling boil. Toss in the spaghetti, stir, return to the boil, and cook until just tender. Drain and return to the pan. Pour over the sauce and stir together. Serve at once; as the sauce is cold, the dish will only be lukewarm.

Spaghetti al Pomodoro

Spaghetti with Tomato Sauce

This is the most typical of all the sauces of Naples, cooked very fast to retain all its colour and flavour and used to dress spaghetti or any other shape of pasta. You do need fresh, ripe, soft tomatoes for this sauce.

Serves 4

1.1kg/2½lb small, soft, ripe, fresh tomatoes
125ml/4fl oz/½ cup olive oil
1 large clove garlic, crushed
salt and freshly milled black pepper
1 teaspoon caster (superfine) sugar
3 tablespoons chopped fresh parsley
400g/14oz spaghetti

Quarter the tomatoes and scoop out the seeds. Fry the seeded tomatoes with their skins in a saucepan with the oil and the garlic over a high heat, stirring frequently. Add the salt, pepper and sugar and continue to cook over high heat, stirring frequently and adding water if the sauce begins to dry out. Do not cover or simmer. Altogether, it needs about 30 minutes to cook, and it should be thick and shiny when finished. Stir in the parsley and leave to stand while you cook the spaghetti.

Bring a large pan of salted water to a rolling boil. Toss in the spaghetti, stir, return to the boil and cook until just tender. Drain well and tip into the pan with the sauce. Mix it all together over a high heat for about 1 minute, then serve at once.

Timballo di Maccheroni al Ragù

Baked Pasta Mould

This is one of those immense dishes with lots of ingredients and many complications. It is probably the ultimate special occasion dish, and is not worth making for any less than eight people. This is an eight-portion quantity, but you can make it bigger if you wish by just doubling up on the ingredients.

In Naples, this dish gets made maybe once a year, for Christmas or New Year, and preparation begins three days in advance. I recommend that you also break up the preparation over three days to lessen the work-load! I promise you, though, it is worth all the trouble!

Serves 8

extra oil for greasing
extra flour for dusting

for the ragù:
300g/10oz veal loin, cubed
500g/1lb pork loin, cubed
500g/1lb pork ribs
125g/4oz lard/½ cup lard, chopped
1 onion, peeled and chopped
2 cloves garlic, chopped
50g/2oz prosciutto crudo (Parma ham), finely chopped
50g/2oz pork dripping
3 tablespoons olive oil
2 tablespoons chopped fresh parsley
5 large leaves fresh basil
2 dried bay leaves
2.5cm/1in sprig fresh rosemary
2.5cm/1in sprig fresh marjoram
2 cloves

½ teaspoon ground cinnamon
salt and freshly milled black pepper
250ml/8fl oz/1 cup dry red wine
400g/14oz/1¾ cups tomato purée (paste)

for the pastry:
400g/14oz/heaped 3 cups plain white (all-purpose) flour
200g/7oz/1 cup caster (superfine) sugar
225g/8oz/1 cup unsalted butter, diced
4 egg yolks
¼ teaspoon salt

for the meatballs:
200g/7oz minced (ground) beef
75g/3oz/¾ cup dried breadcrumbs
25g/1oz/¼ cup grated Parmesan cheese
2 eggs
1 tablespoons chopped fresh parsley
salt and freshly milled black pepper
500ml/¾ pint/2 cups sunflower oil for deep-frying

for the filling:
25g/1oz dried porcini mushrooms
250g/8oz Italian pork sausages
2 tablespoons pork dripping
4 tablespoons dry white wine
1 onion, thinly sliced
50g/2oz pancetta, chopped
250g/8oz fresh peas, shelled, or frozen or canned peas
500g/1lb bucatini or mezzanelli pasta
2 hard-boiled eggs, shelled and sliced
200g/7oz mozzarella cheese, well drained and diced
150g/5oz fresh grated Parmesan cheese
salt and freshly milled black pepper

Spezzatino di Pollo in Bianco/Light Chicken Casserole (page 98), and
Contorno d'Uva/Pan Fried Grapes (page 104)

Day 1:

Make the ragù. Place the meats, lard, onion, garlic, ham, dripping, olive oil and all the herbs and spices in a large flameproof casserole over the lowest possible heat. Season generously with salt and pepper and stir everything together very thoroughly.

After about 2 hours, when the onion is slightly browned, add the wine very gradually, allowing each little bit to boil off its alcohol before adding more. When all the wine has been added and the mixture is heated through and well stirred, remove all the meat with a slotted spoon and set aside.

Raise the heat under the casserole. Add all the tomato purée (paste) and stir it thoroughly into the fat and oil remaining in the casserole. Leave to cook, stirring frequently, until it has gone very dark brown, then add about 4 tablespoons water and stir again. Cover and simmer very gently for 2 hours.

Return the meat to the casserole and continue to simmer it very slowly for a further 2½ hours, stirring frequently. During this time, you may need to skim the fat off the surface from time to time with a slotted spoon, and you may occasionally need to add a tiny amount of water. When it is completely cooked through, dark brown and very thick, leave it to cool completely. Leave the ragù in the refrigerator until you need it, skimming off any surface fat once it is cold.

Day 2:

Make the pastry (dough). Pile the flour on the worktop and make a hollow in the centre with your fist. Put the sugar and butter into the hollow. Add the egg yolks and the salt and knead everything together using the prongs of a fork for as long as possible, then use your fingers to press it into a ball of dough. If you work this pastry too much, it will lose its marvellous crumbly texture, so only knead it for as much as you need to. Wrap the pastry in cling film (plastic wrap) or a plastic bag and put it in the refrigerator to rest for 1 hour.

Grease a 20cm/8in ring mould (12cm/5in deep) very thoroughly, then dust it lightly with flour. Roll out two-thirds of the dough and use it to line the bottom and sides of the mould. Put the mould back in the refrigerator until required. Wrap the remaining dough in cling film or a plastic bag, and keep chilled until it will be used to make the lid for the mould.

Next, make the meatballs. Knead the meat, half the breadcrumbs, the Parmesan, 1 egg, parsley and salt and pepper together to make a tasty meatball mixture. Shape the mixture into meatballs about the size of chestnuts. Beat the second egg thoroughly. Roll the meatballs first in the egg and then in the remaining breadcrumbs.

Heat the oil in a large frying pan (skillet) until a small piece of bread dropped into the oil sizzles instantly. Fry all the meatballs, in batches if necessary, until golden and crisp, then drain well on kitchen paper (paper towels) and set aside.

Day 3:

Make the filling. Cover the mushrooms generously with boiling water and leave them to stand for 1 hour. Drain them, reserving the water. Strain the water through muslin (cheesecloth) to remove any trace of woodland undergrowth, then use the strained liquid to cook the mushrooms until they are completely soft, about 20 minutes. Drain them, then chop them finely and set aside.

Pierce the sausages all over with a needle, then fry them with half the dripping on all sides until browned and cooked through. Pour over half the white wine and allow the alcohol to burn off. Slice the sausages into discs and pour their juices into the ragù but put the sliced, cooked sausages aside until required.

Fry the onion in the remaining dripping with the pancetta. Add the remaining wine and allow the alcohol to burn off for 1 minute before adding the peas. Cover and simmer until the peas are tender, then add the mushrooms, sausage slices and the meatballs. Add about 4 tablespoons of the ragù to this mixture and stir it all together very thoroughly. Simmer over a low heat, stirring frequently, for about 10 minutes. Set aside to cool.

Bring a large pan of salted water to a rolling boil, toss in the pasta, stir and cook until just tender. Drain and return to the saucepan. Pour about one-third of the ragù over the pasta and toss it together very thoroughly. Add half the Parmesan and toss again.

Pre-heat the oven to 190°C/375°F/Gas Mark 5. Use some of this pasta to cover the bottom of the pastry lined mould. Begin to fill the mould, using the ragù, the pea and sausage filling, the hard-boiled eggs, the mozzarella and the remaining Parmesan, creating layers as you go along. You can use the ingredients in whatever order you like, just as long as you make sure there are lots of different layers. Press each layer down with the back of a spoon to make it all fit!

When the mould is full, bang it down firmly on a surface to settle. Roll out the remaining piece of dough to make a lid and lay it on top of the mould. Pinch the edges securely closed all the way around. Pierce the top with a needle in 3 or 4 places to let the steam escape during baking.

Bake for about 20 minutes, or until golden brown. Take it out of the oven and leave it to rest for about 10 minutes. Carefully ease it out of the mould and serve at once.

Turbante di Riso con Gamberi

Rice Ring with Prawns

This is probably one of the most expensive recipes in this book. It is very much a dish for special occasions because it will not just put a strain on your purse, it also requires about four hours hard work and four saucepans! You must use raw prawns (shrimp) for the dish to have sufficient flavour.

Serves about 10

2¼kg/4½lb large raw prawns (shrimp)
1 bouquet garni
175ml/6fl oz/¾ cup dry white wine
salt
1 onion, peeled and finely chopped
1 clove garlic, chopped
125g/4oz/½ cup unsalted butter
2 tablespoons olive oil
3 tablespoons fresh chopped parsley
3 tablespoons brandy
150g/5oz/heaped 1 cup plain white (all-purpose) flour
½ teaspoon paprika
225ml/8fl oz/1 cup single (light) cream
800g/1¾lb/4 cups long-grain rice

The Prawns 1:
Take 30 of the biggest, best-looking prawns (shrimp) and put them to one side. Remove the shells from all the others, reserving all the heads, tails and shells. Remove the vein from the back of each prawn and wipe them clean.

Put the shells into a stockpot with 1.8 litres/ 3 pints (7½ cups) water, the bouquet garni, 2 tablespoons of the wine and ¼ teaspoon of salt.

Bring to the boil then simmer, covered, for 20 minutes. Put all of the reserved unshelled prawns into the boiling water and let them simmer for only 3 minutes, then remove them with a slotted spoon. Shell the cooked prawns and put their heads, tails and shells into the stockpot as well. Keep the cooked prawns to one side.

Simmer the stock for a further 10 minutes, then strain it carefully through a fine sieve (strainer). Put all the shells into the food processor and reduce them to a creamy purée, using a little of the stock to help the process. Sieve this purée through muslin (cheesecloth) and set aside. Keep the stock hot.

The Prawns 2:
In a very large frying pan (skillet), fry the onion and the garlic in one-third of the butter with the olive oil until the onion is soft and transparent. Gradually add the remaining wine to the onion as it fries, allowing the alcohol to boil off as you go along. When the onion is blond coloured, stir in half the parsley. Cook for a further 2 minutes, then add the 30 unshelled raw prawns that you were keeping to one side. Fry them over a fairly high heat for about 4 minutes, stirring frequently to allow the liquid to evaporate from the pan, then remove the prawns and drain them well on kitchen paper (paper towels). Reserve the pan in which they were cooked as you will be using it in a moment to make the sauce.

Put the prawns into a separate pan over a very high heat, pour over the brandy and allow it to ignite, then take the pan off the heat at once. Sprinkle the prawns with salt and set aside, keeping them warm.

The Sauce:
Add half the butter to the pan where the prawns were cooked until it foams, then gradually whisk in the flour, whisking thoroughly. Gradually stir in the hot stock, stirring constantly. Simmer, still stirring constantly, until the sauce reaches the consistency of smooth custard. Sieve (strain) it and return to a very low heat. Stir in the puréed prawn-shell cream, the paprika, the remaining parsley and the single (light) cream. Pour half of this sauce over the prawns which were ignited with brandy and stir gently over a very low heat.

Keeping It All Warm While You Prepare the Rice:
Using 3 saucepans of water on top of the stove with dishes arranged on top like lids, you can use each one to keep the following 3 items warm without cooking them, which will give you time to prepare the rice. Place on top of saucepan 1 the 30 prawns with shells on but without sauce; on top of saucepan 2, the shelled prawns covered in hot sauce; and on top of the third saucepan, the remaining sauce.

The Rice:
In a fourth saucepan, cook the rice in boiling salted water until only just tender. Meanwhile, pre-heat the oven to 140°C/275°F/Gas Mark 1. Lay a clean tea-towel over a baking sheet. Drain the rice very thoroughly, then spread it out on the cloth. Turn the oven off, put the baking sheet in the oven and leave the rice to dry out for 10 minutes.

Use half the remaining butter to very thoroughly grease a 27.5cm/11in ring mould. Take the rice out of the oven and tip it all into a bowl. Add the remaining butter and toss it together with 2 forks. Return the rice to the ring mould, banging the mould down firmly on a work surface to settle the grains. Return the mould to the oven for a further 5 minutes.

Assembling the Dish:
Turn out the rice mould on to a warmed serving dish. Pour the shelled prawns smothered in the sauce into the hole in the centre of the rice ring so they spill out over the top. Arrange the other 30 unshelled prawns around the edges as decoratively as possible. Serve at once with the remaining sauce offered separately.

Fritto Misto/Mixed Fry-up (page 96)

Fritto Misto
Mixed Fry-up

For this recipe, you need to have a well aired space in which to fry all the various ingredients. Any variation, in any quantity, and any combination is acceptable, as long as you have as many different items as possible. You will need at least two deep-fat fryers and some way of keeping all the fried food warm until it is all ready to eat.

Serves 8

15 lemon wedges, to serve

for the batter:
5 eggs
8 tablespoons plain white (all-purpose)
    flour
pinch of salt
750ml/1¼ pint/3 cups milk

frying ingredients:
750g/1½lb small fish, such as whitebait,
    mixed with large raw prawns (shrimp)
1kg/2lb mixed vegetables, such as
    artichokes, very firm tomatoes, peppers,
    courgettes (zucchini) and fennel, all
    trimmed and cut into even-sized pieces
    about 4 x 6cm/2 x 3in
6 sprigs fresh basil
6 sprigs fresh sage
150g/5oz mozzarella cheese, cut into
    chunks
150g/5oz firm ricotta cheese, cut into
    chunks
2.4–3.6 litres/4–6 pints/9–13 cups light
    olive oil or sunflower oil
salt

Make the batter first. Beat the eggs with a balloon whisk until well blended and smooth. Gradually beat in the flour and the salt, beating constantly, then gradually beat in the milk. When you have a lump-free, smooth batter, leave it to stand at least 30 minutes. You may discover that you do not have enough, in which case you will have to repeat this procedure to make more.

Next, prepare the ingredients you are going to fry. Make sure everything is as dry as possible.

Divide the batter into 3 bowls. Put the fish in one, the vegetables in another and the cheese and herbs in the third. Submerge all the ingredients in the batter and let them stand for about 30 minutes.

Divide the oil between 2 or 3 deep-fat fryers and lay out plenty of kitchen paper (paper towels) to absorb the excess oil, putting them on to a large serving platter over a big saucepan of boiling water to keep everything warm without letting the food to go soggy. Heat the oil until a small piece of bread dropped into the oil sizzles instantly. Fry the fish in one pan, and the other ingredients in a second pan and a third pan, if you are using one. Fry quickly, in batches, turning all the ingredients over after about 2 minutes and fishing them out with a slotted spoon as soon as they are golden and crisp. Work quickly and keep the oil at maximum heat so everything can cook as fast as possible. Drain well on the kitchen paper and sprinkle with salt. Serve immediately on a warm platter with the lemon wedges.

Merluzzo ai Capperi

Cod Steaks with Capers

This is a very quick, easy and cheap recipe to make with whole baby cod or with cod steaks. You can use frozen fish for convenience.

Serves 4

1kg/2lb cod steaks, or whole baby cod
    without heads, cleaned
5 tablespoon coarse salt
10cm/4in sprig of fresh parsley
½ onion, peeled
½ lemon
4 tablespoons olive oil
4 tablespoons dried breadcrumbs
2 tablespoons chopped fresh parsley
75g/3oz salted capers, well rinsed, dried
    and finely chopped
2 cloves garlic, sliced into slivers
150ml/¼ pint/⅔ cup dry white wine
extra oil for greasing

Soak the fish in a bowl of water in which the salt has been dissolved for 30 minutes. Meanwhile, pre-heat the oven to 200°C/400°F/Gas Mark 6.

Drain the fish and pat it dry very thoroughly. Fill a saucepan with fresh water. Add the parsley, onion and lemon. Bring to the boil, then simmer for 15 minutes. Add the fish and simmer for 1 minute longer, then remove the fish with a fish slice (pancake turner) and drain. Discard the water.

Lightly oil an ovenproof dish large enough for all the fish to fit in a single layer. Sprinkle with half the oil. Cover the fish with the breadcrumbs, the chopped parsley and the capers. Scatter the garlic on top. Pour the wine around but not on the fish and cover the whole dish loosely with foil.

Bake for 20 minutes, then remove the foil and bake for a further 5 minutes, until the fish flakes easily when tested with the tip of a knife. Serve at once, directly from the baking dish.

Spezzatino di Pollo in Bianco

Light Chicken Casserole

This is a very light dish, quick and easy to make without too many frills. Adapted from an original recipe by the Neapolitan chef Fabrizio Carola.

Serves 4 to 6

750g/1½lb lean boneless chicken, cubed
125ml/4fl oz/½ cup olive oil
1 tablespoon fresh rosemary leaves, or
    1 tablespoon dried rosemary leaves
4 cloves garlic, unpeeled
salt and freshly milled black pepper
5 tablespoons dry white wine
4 potatoes, par-boiled and cubed

Pre-heat the oven to 180°C/350°F/Gas Mark 4. Put the chicken into a large flameproof casserole with half the olive oil. Place over a high heat and seal the chicken all over, sprinkling it with the rosemary, garlic and salt and pepper. When the chicken is well browned, add the wine and cook for a further 5 minutes, then add the potatoes and the remaining oil.

Stir everything together and place the dish in the oven for about 30 minutes, or until both the chicken and the potatoes are brown and crisp on the outside, and the chicken juices run clear if tested with the tip of a knife. Serve at once with a fresh green salad.

Acqua Pazza

Crazy Water

This is an invention of the fishermen of the island of Ponza, who call any dish where the water plays a leading roll: *all'acqua pazza*. Nobody really knows how or why, but the name has stuck and the dish keeps all the delicious flavour of fresh fish intact.

Serves 6

1.3kg/3lb cod, or 6 baby cod, weighing
    250g/8oz each, cleaned
5 tablespoons olive oil
1kg/2lb/5 cups canned tomatoes, well
    drained, seeded and coarsely chopped
2 cloves garlic, chopped
4 tablespoons chopped fresh parsley
1 dessertspoon dried oregano
1 teaspoon salt
1 tiny dried hot red chilli

Rinse the fish and pat dry. Pour 1.8 litres/3 pints/ 7½ cups water into a saucepan big enough to take all the ingredients. Add the oil, tomatoes, garlic, herbs, chilli and salt.

Stir well and bring to the boil. Cover and simmer for 20 minutes, then add the fish and simmer for a further 15 minutes. Transfer to a heated tureen and serve at once.

La Caponata Estiva/Summer Salad (page 101)

L'Insalata Caprese
Tomato and Mozzarella Salad

Be sure to *tear* the basil leaves, not cut them with scissors or a knife as this will blacken the leaves and alter the flavour.

---

2 large beefsteak tomatoes, well rinsed
2 mozzarella cheeses, each the same size as the tomatoes, drained
6 tablespoons olive oil
20 leaves fresh basil, torn into small pieces
salt and freshly milled black pepper
lots of crusty bread for serving

Cut the tomatoes and mozzarella into even sized slices, cubes or chunks. Put them into a salad bowl and mix them together with your hands. Sprinkle with the oil and mix together again with a spoon. Add the basil and sprinkle with salt and pepper to taste and mix again. Leave to stand for about 15 minutes before serving. The juice from the tomatoes and the whey from the cheese will seep out, creating a lot of liquid around your salad. This is delicious and should be soaked up with plenty of crusty bread. When you add salt to the salad, be careful not to add too much as some mozzarella can be quite salty.

Peperoni in Teglia alla Napoletana
Yellow Peppers with Capers

This is one of those lovely dishes which brings together the colours, flavours and textures of the food of southern Italy absolutely perfectly. I prefer to eat these peppers at room temperature, with lots of green salad, bread and cold white wine.

Serves 4

4 tablespoons olive oil
2 cloves garlic, sliced
4 juicy yellow peppers, halved, cored and quartered
1 tablespoon tomato purée (paste)
1 heaped teaspoon salted capers, well rinsed, dried and chopped
3 anchovy fillets, rinsed, dried and chopped
salt

Fry the oil and garlic together until the garlic is browned, then add the peppers. Dilute the tomato purée (paste) with a few tablespoons of water and pour over the peppers. Season with salt, stir, cover and simmer for 15–25 minutes, or until the peppers are soft.

Mix the capers and anchovies together, then stir into the cooked peppers. Cover and leave to stand for about 3 minutes before serving, or serve cold.

La Caponata Estiva

Summer Salad

This is the Campanian variation of the dish which crops up all over the south, in many different forms. There are no actual measurements for the dish, as it is very much a dish which reflects the heat of the summer and the all embracing holiday (vacation) atmosphere. The person who first taught me how to make this said that it was the perfect dish for eating on board a boat, when the sea air begins to make you hungry but you are much too hot to eat a proper meal.

To this basic recipe you can add any of the following: capers, olives, hard-boiled eggs, smoked herrings, sardines, canned tuna fish, Italian pickles, cucumber slices, chopped celery leaves or chopped fresh parsley.

Serves 4

8 *freselle* (dry biscuity bread, ring shaped and often wholemeal), or 8 thin slices stale crusty bread
2 cloves garlic, very thinly sliced
1 heaped teaspoon dried oregano
12 leaves fresh basil, torn into shreds
10 tablespoons olive oil
4 large ripe beefsteak tomatoes, sliced
salt and freshly milled black pepper

Sprinkle the bread very lightly with 4 teaspoons cold water. Mix the garlic, half the dried oregano and half the basil with half the olive oil. Pour this evenly over each of the 4 slices of bread. Sprinkle with salt and freshly milled black pepper.

Mix the tomatoes with the remaining oregano, basil and oil. Season to taste with salt and pepper and cover each slice of bread completely with tomatoes. Leave for at least 1 hour before serving.

Insalata di Rinforzo

Addition Salad

This is a typical dish made to celebrate the Christmas period, and is so called because it has things added to it constantly throughout the period from Christmas Eve, when it is first served, to Epiphany, when it is finally finished off. It is always considered to be at its peak on New Year's Eve.

Serves 4–6

1 cauliflower, washed and trimmed carefully
50g/2oz/⅓ cup black (ripe) olives, stoned (pitted)
50g/2oz/⅓ cup green olives, stoned (pitted)
50g/2oz/⅓ cup pickled gherkins, chopped
50g/2oz/⅓ cup pickled red pepper, well drained and chopped
4 salted anchovies, rinsed, dried boned and cut into thin strips
6–9 tablespoons olive oil
1½–2 tablespoons best quality red wine vinegar
salt

Boil the cauliflower whole in salted water until tender, then cool and divide into florets (flowerets).

Place the cauliflower florets in a salad bowl and add the olives, gherkins and the pickled red pepper. Mix it all together, then add the anchovy strips and mix again. Dress with plenty of olive oil and a little bit of vinegar. Add salt as necessary and leave the salad to chill for at least 1 hour before serving.

Zucchine alla Bella Napoli

Baked Courgettes with Mozzarella and Tomato

Similar to a *Parmigiana di Melanzane*, the ubiquitous vegetarian dish made with aubergines (eggplants), mozzarella and Parmesan cheese in vast quantities, this recipe provides a lighter alternative.

Serves 4

6 courgettes (zucchini), topped and tailed
    and thinly sliced lengthways
salt
1 very small onion, finely sliced
50g/2oz/¼ cup dripping
3 tablespoons olive oil
500g/1lb ripe fresh tomatoes, quartered
    and seeded
5 fresh basil leaves
½ teaspoon dried oregano
300g/10oz fresh mozzarella, drained and
    finely sliced
600ml/1 pint/2½ cups sunflower oil
2 tablespoons plain white (all-purpose)
    flour

Arrange the sliced courgettes (zucchine) on a platter and put it in the sink. Tip it up at one end so the platter remains on a slant and allows the juices from the courgettes to seep out into the sink. Leave them there for about 1 hour.

Meanwhile, fry the onion in the dripping and olive oil until soft, then add the tomatoes, basil and the oregano. Season with salt, cover and simmer for about 45 minutes.

Rinse and pat dry the courgettes. Sieve (strain) the sauce.

Heat the oil until a small piece of bread sizzles instantly. Dust the courgette slices lightly in flour, then fry in the hot oil until golden brown, frying in batches, if necessary. Drain on kitchen paper (paper towels) and set aside. Preheat the oven to 180°C/350°F/Gas Mark 4.

Arrange the courgettes, sauce and mozzarella in layers in a shallow ovenproof dish. Finish off with a layer of tomato sauce. Bake for 20 minutes. Serve hot or cold.

Fagioli alla Maruzzara
Stewed Beans with Tomato, Garlic and Bread

Ideally, you should use fresh white cannellini beans for this dish, but fresh beans are always so hard to get hold of outside of Italy. Dried beans will work equally well, as long as you soak and pre-boil them properly. If you do use fresh beans in their pods, their weight should be 1.2kg/2½lb before shelling.

Serves 4

300g/10oz dried white cannellini beans
1 stick of celery, washed and quartered
500g/1lb ripe fresh tomatoes, peeled,
    seeded and coarsely chopped
2 tablespoons chopped fresh parsley
2 or 3 cloves garlic, chopped
9 tablespoons olive oil
½ teaspoon dried oregano
salt and freshly milled black pepper
8 thin slices stale ciabatta-type bread

Calzone di Mele/Apple-stuffed Pastry (page 105)

Cover the dried beans with cold water and soak overnight.

The next day, rinse the beans and transfer to a saucepan. Cover with fresh water and bring to the boil and boil for about 5 minutes. Drain and rinse thoroughly, then return to the saucepan and cover with abundant fresh water. Bring to the boil, cover and simmer for about 10 minutes. Add the celery and continue to simmer for a further 30 minutes.

Add the tomatoes, parsley, garlic, oil and oregano, season generously to taste and cook for a further 15 minutes, by which time the beans should be mushy. They must not be in any way dry, as the dish is supposed to have the consistency of thick soup. If you feel the beans might be a bit dry, add a little boiling water.

Divide the bread between 4 soup plates and pour the beans over the bread. Serve at once.

Contorno D'Uva

Pan-fried Grapes

In this region, this unusual and rather delicious side dish is often served alongside rich stews and casseroles or heavy game dishes. The slight acidity of the grapes cuts through heavy sauces and any lingering greasiness very well, without leaving any overpowering flavour of its own.

Serves 4

750g/1½lb large Muscat grapes
75g/3oz/5 tablespoons unsalted butter
1 shallot, chopped very finely
1 teaspoon meat extract
2 tablespoons chopped fresh parsley
4 tablespoons dry white wine
salt

Peel all the grapes, then cut them in half and carefully remove all the seeds.

Fry the butter, onion, meat extract and parsley together very gently for about 10 minutes, until the onion is soft and golden. Add the grapes and stir together very gently. Sprinkle with the wine and raise the heat to burn off the alcohol for 2 minutes, gently stirring all the time. Sprinkle with a small pinch of salt and cook for a further 5–10 minutes. Serve at once.

Calzone di Mele

Apple-stuffed Pastry

A lovely apple pastry, shaped like a calzone. This is
also delicious with a pear filling.

Serves 4 to 6

extra flour for dusting
1 egg, beaten, for glazing

for the pastry:
150g/5oz/1 heaped cup plain white (all-
    purpose) flour
75g/3oz/5 tablespoons unsalted butter,
    diced
2 eggs
¼ teaspoon salt
¼ teaspoon icing (confectioners') sugar

for the filling:
350g/12oz apples
2 tablespoons icing (confectioners') sugar
2 tablespoons sweet dessert wine
1 teaspoon ground cinnamon

First make the pastry (dough). Pile the flour on the
work top and make a hollow in the centre with
your fist. Put the butter, eggs, salt and icing
(confectioners') sugar into the hollow and work
into the flour using a fork for as long as it is
possible to do so, then use your fingers to lightly
blend everything together. Make a smooth ball of
dough, wrap it in cling film (plastic wrap), and
chill for at least 1 hour.

Meanwhile, slice the apples thinly, then put
them in a bowl with the icing sugar, wine and
cinnamon. Stir and leave to stand for about 15
minutes. Pre-heat the oven to 180°C/350°F/Gas
Mark 4.

Roll out the pastry on a lightly floured surface
to a circle 35cm/14in across. Arrange the apple
mixture on one half, leaving a generous border all
the way around. Fold it in half and seal the open
edge by pressing with the prongs of a fork.

Glaze lightly with the egg, then carefully slide it
on a baking sheet. Bake for 35 minutes, or until
golden and crisp. Serve hot or cold.

Pizza di Fragole

Strawberry Tart

A wonderful strawberry tart with light custard sandwiched between the delicate layers of crumbly shortcrust (pie crust) pastry. Tricky to make, but magical to eat.

Serves 6

2–3 tablespoons plain white (all-purpose) flour for dusting
25g/1oz/2 tablespoons butter for greasing
1 egg, beaten, for brushing
3 tablespoons icing (confectioners') sugar for decorating

for the pastry:
400g/14oz/heaped 3 cups plain white (all-purpose) flour
200g/7oz/14 tablespoons butter or margarine, cubed
4 egg yolks
grated rind (peel) of 1 lemon

for the filling:
500g/1lb strawberries
200g/7oz/1 cup caster (superfine) sugar
2 tablespoons sweet orange-flavoured liqueur

for the custard:
4 egg yolks
4 heaped tablespoons caster (superfine) sugar
55g/2½oz/heaped ½ cup cornflour (cornstarch)
1 teaspoon vanilla essence (extract)
550ml/18fl oz/2¼ cups milk
grated rind (peel) ½ lemon

Make the pastry (dough) first. Pile the flour on the worktop and make a hollow in the centre with your fist. Put the butter or margarine, egg yolks and lemon rind (peel) into the hollow. Knead together very lightly with your fingertips until you have an elastic, soft ball of dough (without over-kneading!), wrap it in cling film (plastic wrap) or a plastic bag and put it in the refrigerator for 1 hour.

Next, prepare the filling. Mix the strawberries with the sugar and liqueur and put them in the refrigerator to chill for 1 hour.

Meanwhile, make the custard. Using a balloon whisk, beat the egg yolks very thoroughly with the sugar, cornflour (cornstarch) and vanilla in a saucepan. Gradually beat in the milk, beating constantly, then place the saucepan in the top half of a double boiler. Stir constantly until the custard thickens and coats the back of a spoon. Remove from the heat and set aside. Pre-heat the oven to 190°C/375°F/Gas Mark 5.

Drain the strawberries. Divide the pastry into 2 pieces, one slightly larger than the other. Grease a 25–27.5cm/10–11in loose-bottomed tart pan with the butter. Roll out the larger piece of pastry on a lightly floured surface, then use to line the tart pan. Spread the custard all over the bottom, then arrange the drained strawberries on top. Roll out the smaller piece of pastry and use this to make a lid on top of the tart. Seal the edges very carefully by pinching them together with your fingers, and remove any excess bits of pastry with a very sharp knife. Brush thoroughly with the egg.

Bake for about 40 minutes, or until golden brown and crisp. Cool on a wire rack, then remove very carefully from the tart pan. Place on a dish and dust generously with icing sugar before serving.

Puglia

Puglia

Puglia is the 'heel' of Italy's 'boot', a vast and very beautiful region with a long coastline of 760 kilometres and, inland, apparently endless olive groves. The natural beauty and simplicity of the region make it a very popular holiday destination for holiday-makers from all over Italy, and increasingly from the rest of Europe.

Puglia's cuisine provides one of the most perfect examples of the fashionable Mediterranean diet, containing all the elements which make it so healthy and easy to prepare. The simple beauty and intense heat of this region are reflected in the traditional dishes of the lovely 'heel' of Italy.

Puglia's original name was Apulia, when it was inhabited by the Pelasgians and Oscan tribes. Around the eighth century BC it was colonized by the Greeks, especially the city of Taranto, which is where the astronomer known as Philolaus of Tarantum set about expanding and consolidating some of the theories of Pythagoras. His most revolutionary discovery was that the planet Earth is in fact not the centre of the universe.

The region flourished under Roman rule after the defeat of Pyrrhus, but thereafter experienced a very long period of decline under various powers including the Byzantines and the Longobards. At the same time, it was invaded repeatedly by the Saracens. In the eleventh century, the region began to prosper again under Norman rule. Many of the beautiful churches scattered throughout the region belong to this period, and are built in the unmistakably solid style known as Apulian Romanesque. Puglia's most successful era was under the rule of the great Swabian King Frederick II (1220–1250), who divided his beloved kingdom into three separate sections. Throughout Puglia, he built many glorious, solidly proud castles like the Castel del Monte in the province of Bari.

The big maritime cities of Puglia, Taranto, Brindisi and Bari are as busy, polluted and noisy as any industrial city. Fortunately, it is relatively easy to escape from them into the beautiful countryside and remote villages of the interior. Puglia is a region of clearly defined contrasts: this is a land of shepherds and seafarers. From these two very different cultures has evolved a cuisine that is very land based, but which offers an amazing range of fish and seafood once you are on the coast. To polish these dishes to perfection there is the local olive oil, which is green, thick, perfumed and richly pure like no other oil anywhere in the world.

The most startling image of the landscape here has to be the olive groves, which stretch across the softly undulating land literally as far as the eye can see. But not for Puglia the small, gnarled and twisted trees of Tuscany. Olive trees here stand tall and proud, with long branches that spread out wide to give welcome shade from the relentless sun.

Puglia has always suffered from drought, and has the lowest rainfall in Italy. Julius Caesar himself addressed the problem of the region's lack of water nineteen centuries ago. In 1906 the immense building project finally began, and the great Sele Aqueduct was created. This is the largest aqueduct in the world, serving 268 communities, with an output rate of 15 million litres of water per hour! Yet even this is not enough to permit Puglia to fulfil its agricultural potential.

The region divides neatly into four sections: the Gargano, the Tavoliere, the Murghe and the Salentina Peninsula. The Gargano constitutes the northernmost area of the region. It is an area of smooth-topped mountains which descend sharply to a glorious coastline of rocky bays, sandy beaches and tiny islands. Inland lies the huge, rich forest called the Foresta Umbra, from the Latin word *umbra* which means shade.

Moving southwards, you travel across the Tavoliere, Italy's largest peninsular plain. Most of the land is either intensely cultivated or used as pasture. Here stands what is reputed to be the largest pasta factory in Europe, apparently producing eighty per cent of Europe's durum wheat pasta. The grain is driven in at one end, sliding off the tip-up lorries like a rain shower, then travels along the belts, changing from grain to flour, to dough and finally to pasta, and emerging at the other end in packets. The entire process takes just 90 minutes!

In the Murghe lies one the most traditional areas of the entire region. This is rural Puglia at its most evocative. Bitonto, which is famous for producing exceptional olive oil even by Pugliesi standards, is a perfect place to get the flavour of this beautiful region.

Here the olive oil producers will tell you that Cleopatra is supposed to have said to Anthony that 'a man is only a real man if he drinks olive oil', and that the young girls of ancient Greece would say to their boyfriends: 'Bevi olio d'oliva e vieni da me stasera (Drink olive oil and come to me tonight)'. They will also tell you that olive oil has the same molecular structure as human milk, though I don't know if this is why it reputedly makes Pugliesi men so virile!

Further south lie the pretty towns of Alberobello, Crispiano and Locorotondo. All over the wide Valle d'Itria are whole villages made up of *trulli*: white-painted conical houses built out of the stones reclaimed from the soil. *Trulli* are the most traditional feature of rural Puglia and an integral part of the farming communities. What better use for the stones which had to be painstakingly removed from the soil in order to grow their crops than to build a home for the family? When another room is required, or another field needs clearing, the locals simply build on to the existing structure, as they have been doing for centuries.

Crispiano is a tiny little town surrounded by some of the loveliest, most unspoilt countryside I have ever seen. At the town's famous *rosticceria*, you can really get a taste of Puglia's traditional, meat-based cuisine.

In this part of Puglia, a *rosticceria* is the cellar underneath the main butcher's shop in the village or town, which has been cleaned up and made into a simple restaurant. The ceilings are low and domed, and the place is airless and crowded. There is an all pervading smell of singeing meat and wood smoke. It is very noisy and cramped, with a large central fireplace and chimney over which someone (probably the butcher from the shop upstairs) grills the day's leftover meat.

The meat is cooked very simply over a wood fire, with a mere sprinkling of salt. There is horse offal, sheep's offal and goat's offal in great supply, with an occasional chop or small tough strip of meat. And there are so many courses!

In between courses, they serve the traditional local dish called *lo spintone* (which translates, roughly, as the big push). This is a large dish of raw fennel, raw celery sticks, raw carrots and some spring onions, piled high on a dish in very big chunks. There are to be picked up with one's fingers and munched on at leisure. The *spintone* is on offer in restaurants all over the region, and is served either during the meal, or sometimes at the end of a meal in lieu of fruit. It is supposed to encourage you to eat, by pushing the food down to make room for more: hence the name.

Since the days of the Transumanza (the driving of flocks of sheep south from the Abruzzi during the colder months), nomadic tribes of shepherds have existed all over the southern regions. There are about 3,000 kilometres of sheep droves in the Abruzzi, Puglia and Lazio, marking the routes along which the sheep would be led from one area of pasture to another. Although many of them have since fallen out of use, having been taken over by the developing economy, or simply forgotten, some of the nomads and their flocks still use them to this day. With such an ingrained tradition of shepherding, it is not surprising that the cuisine of Puglia, like that of the other regions that lie along the routes of the sheep droves, contains so many dishes using lamb, mutton and kid.

In complete contrast, the coastal areas and, in particular, the bustling fish markets around Bari and Taranto offer the widest selection of seafood anywhere in the country. The Baresi and the Tarantini adore seafood, and prefer to eat it raw! On offer everywhere are raw squid, fresh sea urchins and raw shellfish of every possible shape and variety, from oysters and mussels to gigantic winkles. In the gulf of Taranto are the famous mussel and oyster beds, which supply much of the country. An early morning stroll along the pier of San Nicola in Bari offers real insight into the Pugliese passion for the fruits of the sea. Baskets containing every species of shellfish are displayed all over Taranto, and they can be bought from kiosks, from boats bobbing up and down in the harbour, and from the many knowledgeable fishmongers.

The four elements which make up the cuisine of Puglia are oil, grain, vegetables and fish. Durum wheat flour has always been grown on the Tavoliere plain, and it provides the backbone for the dark, coarse local bread and the infinite number of different kinds of pasta.

Orecchiette are Puglia's favourite pasta shape. As the name suggests, they look like little ears, and they are made by hand with quite extraordinary expertise. In the backstreets of old Bari, women sit in their doorways making them by the hundred. They are then mixed with stewed, fried or boiled vegetables, pulses, olive oil and tomato, or with meat stews for a more substantial one-pot dish.

*Pancotto con Rucola e Patate/Bread Soup with Rocket
and Potatoes (page 112)*

Minestra di Fave Bianche

White Broad Bean Soup

Simplicity is once again the word which typifies this nourishing recipe. In Puglia, rice, or *pastina*, is often cooked separately, then added to this dish to make it even more satisfying. Dried white broad (fava) beans are very characteristic of this region, but dried butter beans or dried green broad beans can be used instead.

Serves 4 to 6

500g/1lb dried white broad (fava) beans
6 tablespoons olive oil
salt

Put the beans into a saucepan, cover with 2.4 litres/4 pints/10 cups cold water and leave to stand overnight and for most of the following day.

The next day, simmer the beans, uncovered, in this water for 45–55 minutes, stirring frequently. When the beans have disintegrated into a smooth creamy texture, season with salt to taste. Stir in the olive oil and serve immediately.

Pancotto con Rucola e Patate

Bread Soup with Rocket and Potatoes

A very simple, peasant dish, with really punchy flavours.

Serves 4

500g/1lb old potatoes, peeled and thickly sliced
salt
500g/1lb rocket (aragula), rinsed and picked over
8 thick slices stale crusty bread
6 tablespoons olive oil
1 clove garlic, lightly crushed
1 small red chilli pepper

Cover the sliced potatoes with cold salted water and bring to the boil, then simmer for about 7 minutes. Stir in the rocket (aragula) and continue to cook until the potatoes are completely soft.

Add the bread and mix it all together very thoroughly.

In a separate pan, heat the oil and fry the garlic and chilli for a few minutes just to flavour the oil. Discard the chilli and garlic. Pour the hot bread soup into a bowl, pour over the hot oil, mix together and serve at once.

Aglio e Olio Pugliese

Pasta with Garlic and Olive Oil

This is one of those incredibly simple dishes which so typify southern Italian peasant-style cookery. The vital ingredients are very fine, highly flavoured olive oil and salted anchovies instead of canned.

Serves 4

400g/14oz vermicelli
3 cloves garlic, crushed
5 tablespoons olive oil
75g/3oz salted anchovies, rinsed, dried, boned and chopped
salt and freshly milled black pepper
3 tablespoons chopped fresh parsley

Bring a large pot of salted water to a rolling boil. Toss in the vermicelli, stir, return to the boil and cook the pasta until just tender.

Meanwhile, fry the garlic in the oil in a saucepan for about 5 minutes, then remove the garlic and add the anchovies. Beat the anchovies to a smooth brown purée in the oil over a low heat. Season with plenty of freshly milled black pepper.

Drain the pasta and tip it into the pan with the anchovy mixture. Mix everything together with 2 forks over the heat, sprinkling on the parsley as you mix. Serve at once, piping hot.

Orecchiette al Pomodoro e Ricotta

Orecchiette with Tomato and Ricotta

Orecchiette are the pride and joy of the local cooks. The word means 'little ears' because they do indeed look like tiny little animal ears. They are made with one part fine semolina to two parts flour and enough hot water to make a kneadable, elastic dough which is then rolled into cylinders and cut into discs. These are then rubbed across the tabletop with a thumb to make slightly concave, thick pasta circles.

Excellent hand-made orecchiette are available in ready to cook form from all good delicatessens and gourmet food shops. The hard ricotta, however, is relatively difficult to get hold of, although most good cheese shops can order it for you if they do not normally stock it. The only possible substitute is a really salty, strongly flavoured hard ewe's milk cheese suitable for grating.

Serves 4

400g/14oz ready made orecchiette
salt
250g/8oz fresh ripe tomatoes, seeded and finely chopped
6 tablespoons olive oil
3 heaped tablespoons hard, mature ricotta, grated

Bring a large pan of salted water to a rolling boil. Toss in the orecchiette, stir, return to the boil and cook for about 15 minutes, or until just tender.

Meanwhile, drain the tomatoes and put them in a saucepan with half the olive oil. Heat through, stirring, for about 10 minutes, then season with a little salt and remove from the heat.

Drain the pasta and transfer it to a warmed serving bowl. Add the tomato sauce, the remaining olive oil and the grated cheese. Toss it all together and serve at once.

Pasta al Cavolfiore

Pasta with Cauliflower

This is a very typical regional dish, reflecting the tradition of cooking vegetables and pasta together in the same saucepan and then adding a simple dressing. This recipe comes from Bitonto, where the olive trees grow tall and thick and the oil is more full of flavour than anywhere else. In other parts of the region, the pasta and cauliflower are finished off with olive oil and freshly milled black pepper rather than with a sauce.

Serves 4

salt and freshly milled black pepper
1 small cauliflower, divided into florets
   (flowerets)
300g/10oz penne or mezze zite
4 tablespoons olive oil
1 large clove garlic, crushed
3 tablespoons chopped fresh parsley
400g/14oz fresh ripe tomatoes, peeled and
   seeded
4 tablespoons freshly grated pecorino
   cheese

Bring a large pan of salted water to a rolling boil. Toss in the cauliflower florets (flowerets) and boil until half cooked for about 5 or 6 minutes. Then toss in the pasta and continue to cook the pasta and the cauliflower until both are tender.

In the meantime, make the sauce. Fry the garlic in the oil until the garlic is golden brown. Add the parsley and stir. Push the tomatoes through a sieve (strainer) and add them to the pan. Season with salt and plenty of freshly milled black pepper.

Drain the pasta and cauliflower and tip into the pan with the sauce. Mix everything together, adding the grated pecorino and a little more black pepper. Heat through and serve at once.

Cozze Ripiene al Sugo

Stuffed Mussels in Tomato Sauce

Slightly more fiddly than some of the other recipes from this region, but actually not nearly as complicated as you might think.

Serves 4

2 cloves garlic, peeled
5 tablespoons olive oil
500ml/¾ pint/2 cups tomato passata
salt and freshly milled black pepper
7 leaves fresh basil, torn into shreds
2 eggs, beaten
2 tablespoons chopped fresh parsley
5 tablespoons fresh breadcrumbs
1 clove garlic, finely chopped
1kg/2lb ready cooked mussels in their
   shells

First, make the sauce. Fry the whole cloves of garlic in the oil until brown, then discard. Add the passata, stir and season. Add the basil and simmer slowly, covered, for about 20 minutes. If necessary, dilute with a little water as you will need enough sauce to cover the mussels completely.

Meanwhile, make the stuffing. Detach the mussels from their shells and set aside. Mix the eggs with the parsley, breadcrumbs and the chopped garlic. Season with salt and pepper and use this mixture to fill the empty shell of each mussel. Close the shell and tie each one closed tightly with a loop of string.

Lay the mussels in the tomato sauce, spooning it over them. Cover and simmer gently for 20 minutes. Remove the string and serve at once.

Cozze Ripiene al Sugo/Stuffed Mussels in Tomato Sauce

Pasta con le Cozze

Pasta with Mussels

The easiest way to enjoy the delicious combinations of pasta with seafood. Please make sure you use really fresh, live mussels, or alternatively mussels which have been cooked while fresh. Do not use mussels in brine or vinegar for this dish. This is a speciality of Campo Marino.

Serves 4

500g/1lb live fresh mussels, or cooked
    mussels in their shells
salt and freshly milled black pepper
350g/12oz spaghetti or maccheroncini
4 tablespoons olive oil
2 cloves garlic, finely chopped
3 tablespoons chopped fresh parsley
400g/14oz fresh ripe tomatoes, peeled,
    seeded, chopped and well drained

If using fresh mussels, scrub and clean all the mussels carefully and rinse them very thoroughly. Discard any that are open. Place the cleaned mussels in a wide frying pan (skillet) and place them over a fairly high heat, shaking the pan frequently to help them open. After about 8 minutes, they should all be open. Discard any mussels which have not opened. Remove all the mussels from the open shells and set aside, carefully wiping off any trace of sand or sediment. Discard the shells.

Bring a large pan of salted water to a rolling boil. Toss in the pasta, stir, return to the boil and cook until just tender.

Meanwhile, heat the oil in a large frying pan (skillet) with the garlic and parsley. Fry for 5 minutes, then stir in the tomatoes. Season and cook over a lively heat for about 8 minutes, stirring occasionally, then stir in the mussels.

When the pasta is cooked, drain it carefully and add it to the pan containing the mussels and tomatoes. Stir it all together and serve at once.

Seppie Ripiene

Stuffed Squid

Like all aspects of Pugliese cuisine, this recipe requires very few ingredients of excellent quality.

Serves 4

1 clove garlic, crushed
4 tablespoons olive oil
6 fresh ripe tomatoes, peeled, seeded and
    chopped
salt and freshly milled black pepper
4 large squid
1 egg, beaten
4 tablespoons dry breadcrumbs
4 tablespoons freshly grated pecorino
    cheese

Fry the garlic in the olive oil for about 5 minutes, until golden. Add the tomatoes and season to taste. Simmer this sauce for about 30 minutes, adding a little water occasionally and stirring frequently. You need to end up with enough sauce to completely cover the squid.

Meanwhile, clean the squid. Make sure you remove the transparent backbones and the inner sacs. Snip off the tentacles and add them to the tomato sauce. Take out the eyes and the beaks. Rinse and dry the squid.

Next, make the filling. Mix the egg with the breadcrumbs and the cheese. Spoon equal quantities into each squid. Do not overfill them as this mixture will swell during cooking. Carefully sew them closed with string. Lower the squid into the sauce, cover and simmer very gently for about 1½ hours, until tender. Serve at once.

Zuppa di Pesce

Mixed Fish Stew

This is the special fish soup which comes from the city of Taranto. Taranto's two seas are incredibly rich when it comes to fish — all manner of seafood, crustaceans and fish, from eels to sea bream, are available at the local markets. It goes without saying, that with such an enormous variety available, the local fish soup (which is rather more like a stew) changes according to seasonal availability, and the weather conditions at sea. Here is one of my favourite versions, which uses fish that are fairly widely available.

Serves 6

1.5kg/3lb total weight after cleaning of a
    mixture of the following: mussels,
    cockles, clams, chunks of huss, chunks
    of cod, squid, raw prawns (shrimp) with
    their shells, raw tiny shrimps with their
    shells and small whole red mullet
8 tablespoons olive oil
3 cloves garlic, chopped
3 tablespoons chopped fresh parsley
9 ripe fresh tomatoes, peeled, seeded and
    sliced into strips
salt and freshly milled black pepper
8 slices ciabatta bread, toasted

Separate the fish as follows: put the chunks of fish, whole small fish, squid, tiny shrimps and prawns (shrimp) in one bowl. Put all the mussels in another bowl. Put any remaining seafood in a third.

Put half the olive oil in a large saucepan with the garlic, half the parsley and half the tomatoes. Fry for about 5 minutes, then add the first bowl of fish. Add 2–3 tablespoons cold water and season. Cover and simmer for about 8 minutes. Take off the heat and leave to one side until required, keeping hot.

Put all the mussels into a second saucepan, cover and shake the pan over the heat for about 6 minutes, or until all the mussels have opened. Discard any that do not open. Carefully strain the liquid from the mussels over the cooking fish. Put the mussels to one side as well, keeping them hot.

Put the remaining oil, parsley and tomatoes into a third pan. Fry gently for 5 minutes, then add all the remaining raw seafood to this pan. Stir, season and simmer for about 6 minutes.

Arrange all the toasted bread in a wide serving bowl and cover with the cooked fish from the first bowl. Scatter the mussels on top, and finally the remaining seafood. Serve at once.

Triglie al Cartoccio
Red Mullet in a Parcel

Baking fish in foil is a cooking method which is used to great effect all over Italy. It has the benefit of retaining all the flavour of the fish and not allowing it to dry out at all during cooking.

Serves 4

4 even-sized red mullet, total weight about 1kg/2lb
salt and freshly milled black pepper
4 teaspoons dried oregano
2 tablespoons chopped fresh parsley
8 tablespoons olive oil
16 stoned black (pitted ripe) olives

Pre-heat the oven to 200°C/400°F/Gas Mark 6. Gut and scale the fish thoroughly, then rinse and dry them. Season generously inside and out. Sprinkle 1 teaspoon of oregano inside each fish.

Oil 4 large squares of foil or baking parchment. Place the fish on top and arrange the parsley and olives on top of each fish. Sprinkle with the remaining olive oil. Bake for 20 minutes, or until the flesh flakes easily. Unwrap and serve at once.

Sfogliata con Olive e Acciughe
Olive and Anchovy Bread

This is a very light loaf with plenty of flavour and a really lovely texture. The traditional way of preparing the dough requires some inbred expertise, so what follows is as close as I can get to the original Pugliese instructions.

Serves 4

for the dough:
400g/14oz/heaped 3 cups white bread (hard) flour
15g/½oz fresh yeast
2 tablespoons olive oil

for the filling:
about 20 green marinaded olives, stoned (pitted)
7 or 8 salted anchovies, rinsed, dried, boned and chopped
12 tablespoons olive oil
freshly milled black pepper

Pile all the flour on the tabletop and make a hollow in the centre with your fist, cream the yeast with just enough water to make a thick liquid, then pour it into the hollow. Add about one-third of the oil and knead together very thoroughly with your hands, making a dough that is as pliable and elastic as possible.

When the dough comes away from your hands, divide it all into small lumps and roll each lump out to a disc approximately the size of a small plate. Put all the discs on to separate plates, cover with cloths and leave them somewhere warm to rise until doubled in size, about 30 minutes. Pre-heat

Sfogliata con Olive e Acciughe / Olive and Anchovy Bread

the oven to 180°C/350°F/Gas Mark 4.

Knock back all the dough and flatten the discs as much as you can. Scatter each disc with a few olives, a few pieces of anchovy and a little olive oil. Roll each disc up loosely to make a tube shape about 3–4cm/7½–10in thick, then push it down from the top to make a kind of rose effect. Place all the squashed tubes side by side in an oiled ovenproof dish. Push them up tight against one another to make one big loaf. Oil the surface and bake for 40 minutes. Excellent either hot or cold.

Peperoni Ripieni

Stuffed Peppers

Traditionally this recipe for stuffed peppers calls for the peppers to be fried in fairly deep olive oil, however, they can also be baked in the oven with less oil.

Serves 4

4 juicy peppers, any colour, rinsed
2 salted anchovies, rinsed, dried, boned and finely chopped
1 heaped tablespoon salted capers, well rinsed and dried
1 heaped tablespoon freshly grated pecorino cheese
2 heaped tablespoons chopped fresh parsley
4 heaped tablespoons fresh white breadcrumbs
2 cloves garlic, finely minced
600ml/1 pint/2½ cups olive oil
salt

Cut off the pepper tops, leaving on the stalks (stems). Mix the anchovies with the capers, pecorino, parsley, breadcrumbs and garlic. Add just enough oil to make a moist texture. Taste and adjust seasoning, if necessary, then use it to fill the peppers. Replace the lids and use 2 wooden cocktail sticks (toothpicks) to keep each lid firmly in place.

Heat the remaining oil and fry the peppers until soft and tender. Alternatively, use only half the remaining oil to grease an ovenproof dish and bake the peppers at 190°C/375°F/Gas Mark 5 for 35 minutes, or until soft. Serve piping hot.

Zucchine alla Poverella

Poor Woman's Courgettes

There are lots of different ways of preparing this recipe, which is one of the most traditional Pugliese dishes. It is called *alla poverella* because the ingredients required for the dish are cheap and easily available, indeed most people who grow their own courgettes (zucchini) in Puglia will also have their own garlic and mint growing in the garden, and a cellar full of oil, wine and vinegar.

Serves 4

8 courgettes (zucchini), rinsed and topped and tailed
225ml/8fl oz/1 cup olive oil
salt
12 leaves fresh mint, coarsely chopped
150ml/5fl oz/⅔ cup light red wine vinegar
2 large cloves garlic, chopped

Slice the courgettes (zucchini) lengthways into thin strips. Heat the oil until just smoking, then fry the courgette strips in the oil for about 4 minutes on either side, until softened and golden. Drain the courgettes well on kitchen paper (paper towels). Arrange them in layers in a dish, sprinkling with salt and about half the mint as you arrange them.

Pour the wine vinegar into a saucepan and add about ⅛ teaspoon of salt and the remaining mint. Bring to the boil, then simmer for about 5 minutes. Pour this hot marinade all over the courgettes. Leave to stand until cool. Serve slightly chilled.

Frittelle di Patate

Potato Fritters

Deliciously simple cheesy fritters, these are best served piping hot. These are especially wonderful with grilled (broiled) Italian sausages and a mixed green salad for a really satisfying lunch or family supper.

Serves 4

500g/1lb old potatoes, peeled
2 tablespoons freshly grated pecorino cheese
2 tablespoons plain white (all-purpose) flour
¼ teaspoon salt
¼ teaspoon freshly milled black pepper
2 eggs, beaten
1 litre/1¾ pints/4½ cups sunflower oil

Grate the potatoes coarsely into a bowl. Stir in the cheese, flour and seasoning. Pour over the eggs and mix together very thoroughly.

Heat the oil until a small piece of bread dropped into it sizzles instantly. Drop large spoonfuls of the potato mixture into the hot oil and fry on both sides until crisp and golden. Scoop out of the hot oil and drain thoroughly on kitchen paper (paper towels) before serving.

Dita d'Apostoli

Apostles' Fingers

Once you see what these pastries look like, you will know where they get their name!

Makes 12

225g/8oz/1 cup fresh ricotta cheese
100g/3½oz/½ cup caster (superfine) sugar
50g/2oz/½ cup cocoa powder, sifted
3 tablespoons sweet white liqueur, such as Sambuca, sweet grappa, or Maraschino
4 egg whites, chilled
50g/2oz/¼ cup butter
3 tablespoons sunflower oil
¼ teaspoon salt
4–6 tablespoons icing (confectioners') sugar, sifted

Blend the ricotta, sugar, cocoa powder and liqueur together to make a smooth amalgamated paste. Beat the egg whites until fluffy and white, but not stiff. Beat in the salt.

Heat a 10–12cm/4–5in frying pan (skillet) with a little of the butter and a little of the oil. Spoon one-twelfth of the egg white into the pan and fry it quickly on both sides to make a sort of pancake (crêpe). Continue in this way, greasing the frying pan in between each pancake, until all the egg whites have been used up. As soon as each pancake is ready, lay it on to kitchen paper (paper towels) to drain a little, then fill the centre with the ricotta mixture and roll up the pancake around the filling to make a thick finger shape. It is very important to do this while the pancakes are still hot and it will help if you have your hands slightly wet. As soon as you have rolled them all up, dust generously with icing (confectioners') sugar and serve. These pastries are excellent either warm or chilled.

Mustazzueli

Almond Biscuits

These almond biscuits (cookies) are very hard when you first attempt to bite into them, but once in your mouth they become very crumbly and incredibly moreish! They are fantastic with chilled dessert wine.

Makes about 12

250g/8oz/1⅓ cups whole blanched almonds
350g/12oz/2¾ cups plain white (all-purpose) flour, sifted twice
250g/8oz/1¼ cups sugar
75 ml/3fl oz/⅓ cup cold water

Pre-heat the oven to 200°C/400°F/Gas Mark 6. Scatter the almonds all over 1 or 2 baking sheets and toast them in the oven for 5 minutes, until golden brown. Take the almonds out of the oven, but leave the oven switched on.

Put the toasted almonds in the food processor and grind them to a fine powder. Pile three-quarters of the flour on the worktop and make a hollow in the centre with your fist. Pour the ground almonds into the hollow. Put the sugar and the water in a small saucepan and stir over a low heat until the sugar melts and the mixture becomes a smooth syrup. Cool slightly, then pour the syrup into the hollow. Mix the syrup into the flour and almonds with your hands, working quickly to achieve a smooth and elastic dough. Scatter half the remaining flour on to the work surface and roll the dough out in a cylinder with a diameter of about 3cm/1½in.

Cut it into even-sized discs with a sharp knife, then flatten each one out with the palm of your hand so you reduce the thickness of each one to about 5cm/¼in. Cut each of the flattened discs into squares using a 3.5cm/1½in biscuit (cookie) cutter.

Use the remaining flour to dust 1–2 baking sheets. Arrange the finished biscuits (cookies) in rows on the baking sheets. Bake for 10–15 minutes, until golden brown. Remove them quickly from the sheets using a palette knife (metal spatula) and arrange them on wire racks to cool. Store in air tight containers if not served immediately.

Basilicata

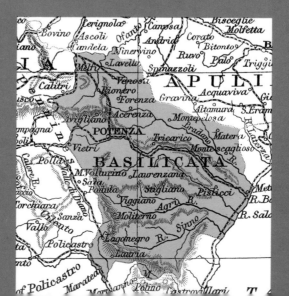

Basilicata

The small region of Basilicata is situated between the gulf of Taranto, the Tyrrhenian coast and the Apulian lowlands. Much of the landscape is either mountainous and craggy or else densely wooded, making communication between one area and another at best difficult and in some places virtually impossible. Isolation, neglect and lack of development make this one of Italy's poorest regions. There is very little industry, though wherever possible in this barren land there are fields under cultivation, providing fruit and vegetables for export all over Europe. Although the raw, bald, almost lunar landscape is fascinating in its own way, one cannot help wondering what it must be like to live and work in an area which is now as desolate as this one.

It wasn't always like this. Basilicata, like the rest of the south, had its finest hour when it was part of Magna Graecia. Between the eighth and the fourth century BC, the strip of coastline along the Gulf of Taranto was colonized by Greeks from the area near the port of Patrai. At Metaponto, Pythagoras set up his school of philosophy. Although he is probably best remembered as a mathematician, Pythagoras actually spent most of his time running an extremely powerful political brotherhood. The school and the great man's tomb have long since disappeared, but there are still a few scanty remains of various temples, and a Greek theatre from the fourth century BC. Nearby are the ruins of the Temple of Hera (the goddess of fertility), dating from the sixth century BC, and at Policoro the ruins of the city of Heraclea, built in the fourth century BC, can also be seen.

Gradually the Greek colonies began to be occupied by the Lucanians, who lived in the much more inaccessible inland areas of the region. In the centuries that followed, the region was drawn into Rome's struggles with the Samnites and the campaigns against Pyrrhus and Hannibal, and slipped further into decline. The situation got worse with the various Barbarian invasions, and under the rule of the Longobards, who took over in AD 847, malaria became rife and the population dwindled as people either died or went away to begin a new life elsewhere. Under Byzantine rule, the region was renamed Basilicata, after the Emperor Basil II, who overthrew the Saracens in Sicily and southern Italy and ruled here from 976 to 1025.

Midway through the eleventh century, the first royal Norman nucelus was set up at Melfi. The Normans appear to have attached great value to this city, which is on top of a rather beautiful volcanic hill at the feet of the Vulture mountain. Virtually all of the original Norman wall remains intact, as well as one of the gateways and the original square Norman castle which dominates the whole town. On the ground floor of the castle is the national Museum of Melfi, which contains many local archeological finds. On the hilltops around the town are churches decorated with lovely thirteenth-century Byzantine frescoes.

The Angevins, who took over from the Normans, also seem to have had a great affection for the region, and for Melfi in particular, but as political fervour in Naples grew, Basilicata was almost completely forgotten and abandoned to her fate. For the next six or seven centuries, Basilicata continued to exist in complete isolation from the rest of the country, all the political activity outside her borders scarcely impinging on the daily life of the region. For example, Masaniello's attempted revolt against taxation and the setting up of his Parthenopean Republic in 1647 was more like a story from a far away country than a political event which might affect Basilicata. Nothing seemed to penetrate the torpor into which the region had slipped: not the cultural renewal, influenced very much by France, which occurred elsewhere during the eighteenth century, not the whispered rumour of revolution which snaked its way through the south from 1815.

Basilicata, like the beauty in a fairy tale, went on sleeping sadly until 1860, when she was finally united with the rest of Italy. By that time her forests had been stripped by the British shipbuilding industry, the trees sold by the locals to make room for fields of crops to feed their hungry families. This in turn has caused the region's most serious modern problem: soil erosion.

Malaria, cholera and other diseases also afflicted the region until as recently as about 1960, and flooding, earthquakes and drought are almost everyday occurrences. There was and still is much to be done to improve the general living conditions of this 'land forgotten by God'.

The region's two main towns are Potenza and Matera, each presiding over its respective province. There are very few isolated houses to be found anywhere, and most of the little villages are scattered far apart and are often found huddled at the foot of an ancient ruined castle. The grinding poverty of this region has pushed people to emigrate all over the world – they say there are more Lucani (as the people are still called) living outside the region than there are here.

The ancient city of Matera is like an anthill and is one of the most fascinating archeological sites I have ever visited. The first inhabitants of the area set up their encampments 5,000 years ago, using natural cavities in the rocks and gradually the settlements expanded until all the tunnels, alleys, caves, tiny squares and hollows had taken over a vast hilly area and become a complete city.

It is hard to imagine what it must have been like for an entire population to live within this labyrinth of tunnels. Yet convents existed here, as well as churches and palaces and simple family homes. In the 1950s the oldest part of the city was evacuated for reasons of hygiene and the entire place was restored. It is now a pristine, ancient ghost town, waiting for everybody to come home.

Despite its tortured history, geological nightmares and lack of incentive, there is always solace to be found in eating and drinking, and even this region has come up with a range of specialities and traditional dishes which have a very special identity. This brings us to the other thing which Matera is famous for: its extraordinary, vast loaves of pale yellow bread. These loaves are so enormous (the average weight is about 5 kg) because when the villagers and townspeople had to take their dough to a central, communal oven for baking, they were charged by the loaf irrespective of the weight. So the Lucani, wily and hungry, would make their loaves as big as possible – but they had to find a way of stopping all this bread from going stale. The addition of maize meal to the wheat flour solved the problem and also gave the bread its characteristic yellow colouring.

Bread is so much a part of the local cuisine that it is used in a host of different dishes. It is soaked in egg, flavoured with herbs and deep fried to make golden 'bread balls', fried crumbs are sprinkled over pasta, and it is used to stuff vegetables and poultry and added to other more expensive ingredients just to make everything go a bit further. In Matera, the words 'Staff of Life' have more meaning than elsewhere.

All over the region, the traditional cuisine is based on the few, simple ingredients available such as mutton, goat, dried salt cod, pulses, grain in various forms and some game. All these are served alongside pasta in hundreds of different shapes and sizes and various vegetable dishes.

The one thing which has always appeared to grow without any problem at all in this barren, arid soil is the chilli pepper – the *peperoncino* or *diavollillo*, as they call it here. The chilli is liberally added to all kinds of dishes, but is also used as a special condiment called *olio santo*, or holy oil, which is nothing more complicated than several chillis crushed into a bowl of olive oil and left to steep for several weeks until the oil is practically black. The name derives from the fact that it was supposed to cure all kinds of illness, from cholera to the plague.

A feast in Basilicata is as satisfying and delicious as food anywhere in the south, even though the range is rather restricted, compared with that of Sicily or Naples. There is, for example,

an excellent mutton casserole which is placed to bake at the mouth of a wood-burning oven in a terracotta pot with the opening sealed by raw bread dough or a few handfuls of mud. This goes back to the time when it was the custom to bake things in the glowing embers of an outdoor fire. It consists of nothing more than chunks of meat, potatoes, onion, celery and tomatoes, flavoured with the inevitable chilli and sometimes finished off with a generous handful of grated pecorino. The finished dish is superbly tender and packed with flavour.

Basilicata only has three wines of any note, as vineyards have a hard time struggling against the elements. Aglianico, which has been made here since the time of the Ancient Greeks, is an intense red wine that is very good to drink with full flavoured meat dishes, mature cheeses and game. It is characterized by a strong scent of violets and a foamy surface. The other two wines that are produced here, Malvasia del Vulture and Moscato del Vulture, are both white and named after the mountain which dominates the region. The Malvasia is a good table wine which goes well with seafood and fish and with vegetable dishes and simple soups. Pale, golden yellow in colour, it has a lovely almondy nose. The Moscato is a rich dessert wine to sip slowly with the locally made pastries and cakes.

Lagane e Fagioli / Home-made Pasta with Beans (page 129)

Frittelle di Semolino

Semolina Fritters

I am sure these fritters would evoke memories of childhood for many Italians who grew up in this region, or indeed anywhere in the country. I can remember long afternoons when huge piles of piping hot fritters of one sort or another were preparing for our *merenda*, the afternoon children's snack which was supposed to see you through the hours between lunch and supper and was consumed with much gusto after siesta!

Makes about 14

250g/8oz/2 cups plain white (all-purpose) flour

200g/7oz/1¼ cups fine semolina

3 tablespoons olive oil

¼ teaspoon salt

¼ teaspoon ground cinnamon

1 bay leaf

2 cloves

1.8 litres/3 pints/7½ cups sunflower oil for deep-frying

6 tablespoons icing (confectioners') sugar mixed with 1 teaspoon ground cinnamon

Pour 850ml/1½ pints/3¾ cups cold water into a deep saucepan and gradually trickle in the flour and semolina, beating constantly to avoid lumps. Add the oil, salt, cinnamon, bay leaf and cloves. Bring to the boil, then simmer gently, beating constantly to avoid lumps, over a low heat until the mixture comes away from the sides and results in a soft, compact, smooth mass.

Tip it out on to a lightly oiled work top and spread it out to cool. It should be no thicker than 1cm/½in. Cut into squares.

Heat the oil in a deep-fat fryer until a small piece of bread dropped into it sizzles instantly. Fry all the squares until golden and crisp, then drain them thoroughly on kitchen paper (paper towels). When they are all cooked, sift the icing (confectioners') sugar mixed with the cinnamon over them. Arrange on a warm dish and serve hot.

Pasta al Ragù di Potenza

Pasta with Potenza Sauce

Potenza is a fairly remote kind of town, notable for having the lowest and highest temperatures anywhere in Italy! This pasta sauce, which is used to dress all kinds of pasta shapes from spaghetti to ravioli, is definitely one of Potenza's most redeeming features.

All over the region, one-pot dishes keep appearing, where the pasta sauce is cooked with large, chunky pieces of meat. This means that the pasta and the sauce make a very filling, nourishing first course and the meat can go on to be the second course or even a separate meal. As a reflection of the lean nature of the local dishes, this sauce is traditionally used to dress a bowlful of soaked, boiled wheat grains to make a dish called simply *Grano al Ragù*.

Serves 6

2 cloves garlic, chopped

3 tablespoons chopped fresh parsley

¼ teaspoon chilli powder

¼ teaspoon grated nutmeg

25g/1oz/¼ cup grated pecorino cheese

25g/1oz/¼ cup finely cubed pecorino cheese

1 large single slice pork or beef, weighing about 600g/1¼lb, such as beef skirt, or a boned pork hand or shoulder, skinned

75g/3oz pancetta, thinly sliced

salt

2 tablespoons lard or dripping

3 tablespoons olive oil

5 tablespoons dry white wine

500g/1lb/2½ cups canned tomatoes, drained, seeded and chopped

600g/1¼lb fresh pasta of your choice

Put the garlic and parsley into a small bowl with the chilli powder, nutmeg and grated and cubed cheese. Mix all this together very thoroughly.

Flatten the meat as much as possible with a meat mallet, trimming off any fat or gristle. You need to end up with a fairly even, relatively thin sheet of meat which can then be rolled up on itself.

Line the meat completely with the pancetta. Spread the garlic, parsley, chilli and cheese mixture all over the pancetta, sprinkle with salt and roll up. Tie closed securely.

Melt the lard or dripping with the oil in a deep frying pan (skillet) or flameproof casserole. Lie the roll of meat in the hot fat and seal it all over. Pour in the wine and boil off the alcohol for about 3 minutes, turning the meat frequently. Add the tomatoes, sprinkle with a little more salt and cover. Simmer very slowly for about 3 hours, adding a little water occasionally.

Bring a large pan of salted water to a rolling boil. Toss in the pasta, stir, return to the boil and cook the pasta until just tender. Drain well. Remove the meat roll from the sauce and set aside. Pour the pasta into the sauce, toss together and transfer on to a platter to serve.

Lagane e Fagioli

Home-made Pasta with Beans

On the 19th March, St Joseph's Day, the smaller communities throughout the entire region make vast quantities of *lagane* and distribute them among those who are less fortunate. You will need fresh borlotti, cannellini or haricot beans for this dish. Almost exactly the same dish can be made with whatever pulse happens to be available, even fresh broad (fava) beans.

Serves 6

500g/1lb fresh beans in pods
600g/1¼lb/4¾ cups plain white (all-
    purpose) flour
salt
2 tablespoons dripping
2 large cloves garlic, lightly crushed
¼ teaspoon crushed dried chillies

Shell the beans and place them in a saucepan.
Cover with water and boil gently for about
45 minutes, or until tender. Add salt only at the
end of the boiling time otherwise the skins will
toughen.

Meanwhile, make the pasta. Place all the flour
on the worktop and make a hollow in the centre
with your fist. Add a little salt and gradually add
enough water as you knead to make a smooth and
elastic dough. You will need time and considerable
energy to get the dough to the right texture so that
you can finally roll it out to a fine sheet.

Roll out the dough as thinly as possible, then
cut it into 2.5cm/1in strips with a sharp knife or a
pastry wheel. Leave the pasta strips to dry for
about 15 minutes.

Bring a large pan of salted water to a rolling
boil. Toss in the pasta, stir, return to the boil and
cook the pasta until just tender.

Meanwhile, fry the dripping with the garlic and
the chilli for about 10 minutes over a gentle heat.
Drain the beans and keep them hot. When the
pasta is tender, drain it well and transfer it to a
warmed serving bowl. Add the oil and the beans.
Mix everything together and serve at once.

Piatto di Verdure alla Lucana

Lucanian Vegetable Stew

Basilicata is still Lucania to many of its inhabitants,
and many of the dishes still bear the name of
Lucania as a kind of proof of authenticity! The
vegetables that grow in these arid fields have a
flavour and a scent which is quite unique.

Serves 6

2 aubergines (eggplants), rinsed and cubed
salt
3 large onions, peeled and thinly sliced
25g/1oz/½ cup fresh basil leaves
25g/1oz/½ cup fresh flat-leaf parsley
3 cloves garlic, peeled
5 tablespoons olive oil
2 large yellow peppers, cored, seeded and
    cut into strips
4 small ripe tomatoes
1 loaf ciabatta bread, sliced thinly and
    toasted, to serve

Sprinkle the aubergines (eggplants) with salt and
place them in a colander with a heavy plate on top.
Put the colander in the sink and leave them to
drain for 30 minutes. Meanwhile, peel the
tomatoes by dipping them in boiling water, then
cut them in half and discard the seeds. Chop the
basil, parsley and garlic together.

Pour the olive oil into a saucepan large enough
to take all the vegetables. Add the onions and fry
very gently over a low heat, until soft and lightly
browned. Rinse and pat dry the aubergines, then
add them to the onions. Stir and cook for about

Piatto di Verdure alla Lucana/Lucanian Vegetable Stew

5 minutes, then add the peppers and tomatoes. Stir, season with salt, cover and leave to simmer for about 10 minutes. Add the chopped herbs and garlic and stir again, then simmer, uncovered, for about 1 hour, stirring frequently. Serve hot or cold, accompanied by the warm toasted ciabatta.

Minestra Strascinata

Home-made pasta with tomato and pecorino

Making this type of pasta is a real testimony to the devotion, strength and energy of the local cooks. Real muscle power is needed to make these tiny strips which are so typical of the local cuisine. Ideally, you need to use a *chitarra*, a guitar-like cooking instrument used in the Abruzzi to make the region's kind of pasta, but a normal hand-turned pasta machine will cut the pasta strips into spaghetti, or alternatively you can use a sharp knife, a steady hand and a sharp eye! This is a recipe from Potenza.

Serves 4

400g/14oz/heaped 3 cups plain white (all-purpose) flour
½ tablespoon lard or dripping, diced
salt
2 cloves garlic, lightly crushed
4 tablespoons olive oil
3 tablespoons tomato purée (paste) diluted in 300ml/½ pint/1¼ cups lukewarm water
125g/4oz/1 cup freshly grated pecorino cheese

Pile all the flour on the tabletop and make a hollow in the centre with your fist. Add the lard or dripping, and ¼ teaspoon salt, and begin to knead energetically, gradually adding as much water as you need to make an elastic and rather tough dough. You will need at least 40 minutes to achieve this, and lots of stamina.

When the dough is as workable as possible, roll it out on the tabletop. Cut it into narrow, square spaghetti, using one of the methods mentioned in the introduction. Then cut the spaghetti across the other way to make tiny cubes. Leave them to dry out while you prepare the sauce.

Fry the garlic lightly in the oil for about 5 minutes. Add the diluted tomato purée (paste) and stir. Season with salt and leave to simmer for about 30 minutes.

Bring a large pan of salted water to a rolling boil. Toss in the pasta, stir, return to the boil and cook until just tender. Please note that the characteristic of this type of dough is that the pasta will always remain slightly firm (*al dente*) however much you boil it. When it is cooked to the right point for you, drain it very thoroughly and tip it into a warmed tureen. Add the sauce and the cheese and mix it all together. Serve at once.

Lagane e Ceci

Home-made Pasta with Chick-peas

This recipe, like Home-made Pasta with Beans (page 129), reflects the grinding poverty of this incredibly remote region. The availability of local ingredients has always been extremely limited – what could not be cultivated or bred in the severe climatic conditions of Basilicata simply did not exist. Even now, road, rail and air communications to the region are minimal, and the unavailability of many ingredients is a constant reminder of the fact that one is in a land in which time seems all but forgotten.

Serves 6

500g/1lb/2½ cups dried chick-peas
600g/1¼lb/4¾ cups plain white (all-
    purpose) flour
salt
5 tablespoons olive oil
2 cloves garlic, finely chopped
½ onion, peeled and sliced

Soak the chick-peas overnight in plenty of cold water. Drain well, then cover with fresh water. Bring to the boil and boil quickly for about 5 minutes. Drain and cover with fresh water, then simmer slowly for about 3 hours, or until soft and tender. Season the chick-peas with salt only when they are soft enough to eat. Meanwhile, make the lagane as described on pages 129–30).

Fry the oil, garlic and onion together gently until the onion is soft and golden brown. Bring a large pan of salted water to a rolling boil. Add the lagane, stir, return to the boil and cook until just tender. Drain well and transfer to a warmed serving bowl. Add the chick-peas and the fried onion and garlic, toss everything together. Serve at once.

Strascinati con Pomodoro e Cavolfiore Verde

Home-made Pasta with Tomato and Green Cauliflower

Strascinati literally means 'dragged', which is the word used to describe the technique of dragging the pasta across the table to make it the right shape so it cooks evenly and surrounds itself with the maximum amount of dressing or sauce. You will need to work on a rough wooden tabletop to achieve the right effect. Very similar versions of this dish exist all over southern Italy, but the day I was given this particular version for my lunch, was on the occasion of my first visit to the all but abandoned, extraordinary, eerie and ancient city of Matera. It is a day I shall never forget.

Serves 6

600g/1¼lb/4¾ cups plain white (all-
    purpose) flour
salt
1 green Romanesco cauliflower, divided
    into florets (flowerets)
3 cloves garlic, thinly sliced
¼ teaspoon crushed dried red chilli pepper
6 tablespoons olive oil
500g/1lb/2½ cups canned tomatoes,
    drained and seeded
4 tablespoons pecorino cheese, grated

Make the pasta first. Pile all the flour on the tabletop and make a hollow in the centre with your fist. Add a little salt and then gradually tip enough water on to your hands and knead the dough energetically until you achieve a smooth and elastic texture. This will take time and energy. When the dough forms a smooth and elastic ball, divide it into smaller balls. Roll out each ball on the tabletop into a snake shape. Cut each snake into even-sized pieces of about 3cm/1¼in each. Roll each section across the table to lengthen it, then coil it up again. Do not be too worried about making them look too tidy. When all the *strascinati* are ready, lay them on to a lightly floured surface to dry out for 5 to 10 minutes. Bring a large pan of salted water to a rolling boil, then toss in the cauliflower florets (flowerets). Boil until tender, then remove the cauliflower and keep warm. Toss the pasta into the same water, stir and boil it until just tender.

Meanwhile, fry the garlic and the chilli in half the oil, in a very big saucepan, for about 5 minutes, then add the tomatoes. Season with salt and simmer for 15–20 minutes.

When the pasta is tender, drain well. Tip the pasta into the sauce and add the cauliflower. Mix it all together and heat through, transfer to a warmed serving platter. Finally sprinkle with the cheese and serve at once.

Beccaccini in Salmì

Snipe Casserole

The little snipe is a very delicious bird, but you must be patient enough to fiddle around with all its tiny bones. To be certain, there is not a lot of meat on a snipe, but the meat has a unique and exceptionally delicious flavour. The birds need to be hung for two or three days before gutting and plucking carefully. This is another recipe from the city of Potenza.

Serves 4

4 snipe, plucked and cleaned with innards reserved and trimmed
salt and freshly milled black pepper
4 large slices of prosciutto crudo (Parma ham)
6 tablespoons olive oil
1 small wine glass dry white wine
1 small wine glass sweet Marsala
1 heaped tablespoon salted capers, rinsed and drained
2 large salted anchovies, boned, rinsed and patted dry
½ loaf ciabatta bread, sliced and toasted

Strangolapreti Fritti / Fried Priest Stranglers (page 137)

Make sure the snipe are perfectly clean, then season them inside and out with salt and the freshly milled black pepper. Wrap them securely in the ham, using a wooden cocktail stick (toothpick) to make sure the ham does not slip off. Pour 4 tablespoons of the oil in a wide frying pan (skillet) and heat until gently sizzling. Lay the birds in the hot oil and seal them all over until lightly browned. Sprinkle with half the white wine and half the Marsala, then boil off the alcohol for about 2 minutes. Lower the heat, cover and leave the snipe to cook gently for about 15 minutes, or so.

Meanwhile, rinse the reserved innards very carefully and chop them very finely with the capers and the anchovies. Pour the remaining olive oil into a separate pan and add the chopped mixture. Fry gently for about 5 minutes, stirring frequently. Pour over the remaining white wine and Marsala and continue cooking slowly for about 10 minutes.

Spread this mixture, over the slices of toasted bread and arrange them on a warmed platter. Place a snipe on top of each, drizzle the juices from the pan all over and serve at once.

Orecchiette con Aglio e Peperoncino in Padella
Sautéed Orecchiette with Garlic and Chilli

Orecchiette are borrowed from next door Puglia for this incredibly fiery hot dish. Because the sauce is so very hot, the very thick quality of this type of pasta acts as a very bland counterfoil.

Serves 4

salt
400g/14oz orecchiette
150ml/¼ pint/⅔ cup olive cup
3 cloves garlic
4 whole dried red chillies
4 tablespoons tomato purée (paste)

Bring a large pan of salted water to a rolling boil for the pasta.

Meanwhile, heat the oil gently in a very large pan with the garlic and chilli. Fry until the garlic is soft and golden brown and the chilli pepper is very shiny and swollen. Do not let either burn.

Scoop the garlic and the chilli out of the oil and put in the food processor with the tomato purée (paste). Process until smooth, then stir back into the remaining oil in the pan. Toss the pasta into the boiling water, stir, return to the boil and cook until just tender. Drain well and tip into the pan. Stir together quickly over a medium heat, sprinkling with the remaining oil. Serve at once.

Cipolle Fritte con Capperi

Fried Onions with Capers

I remember eating this very simple side dish as part of an endless buffet at a small *trattoria* in Matera. What struck me most about it then, and it does again now as I re-create the flavour of the dish, is how absolutely nothing in the cooking of this region is bland or delicate. All the flavours assault you, firing up your belly and sending your taste-buds into tingling action. Even the bread, though not peppery or particularly salty, has a kind of potency of its very own. I find this is a very good accompaniment for dishes of boiled meat.

Serves 6

4 tablespoons olive oil
3 large, strong-tasting onions (the kind which really make your eyes water), peeled and thinly sliced
1 tablespoon chopped fresh mint
125g/4oz/¾ cup salted capers, well rinsed, drained and chopped
salt and finely crushed chillies

Put the oil into a frying pan (skillet) and heat slowly. Add the onions and fry them gently until softened, then raise the heat and stir them quickly to brown them slightly all over.

Take the pan off the heat and stir in the mint and capers and season with salt and crushed chillies to taste. Cool before serving.

Strangolapreti Fritti

Fried Priest Stranglers

The story of the priest strangler has many different versions, depending upon where you are in Italy. The one I like the best is that when the priest came to call, the household cook would prepare this speciality for him in his honour and that he would be so greedy and stuff himself so much that he would end up choking himself!

Serves 4

300g/10oz/3 cups fine white flour (cake flour)
3 eggs
¼ teaspoon salt
grated rind (peel) of 1 lemon
1.8 litres/3 pints/7½ cups light olive oil for deep-frying

Pile all the flour on the worktop and make a hollow in the centre with your fist. Break the eggs into the hollow and add the salt and the lemon rind (peel). Knead everything together fairly energetically to make a reasonably firm dough. Wrap it in a towel to rest for 10 minutes.

Divide the dough into sections and roll out each section on the worktop like a cylinder, the same size and shape as short grissini. Cut each cylinder into sections no longer than 2–3cm/¾–1¼in. Roll these against the back of a cheese grater to make them concave on one side and to mark them with the grooves of the grater on the other side. When they are shaped, lay them on a worktop to dry.

Heat the oil until a small piece of bread dropped into it sizzles instantly. Fry all the dough shapes until puffy and golden. Drain well on kitchen paper (paper towels) and serve at once, with plenty of wine.

Copete

Almond Pastries

This recipe would have originally used real hosts, as used for communion in church, but in case you cannot get hold of any, sweet shops do sell oblongs of 'edible paper' of various colours. These can be cut into circles and used instead. The use of the hosts is typical of the tradition of delicate pastry making carried out in convents by the nuns, where hosts were presumably in ample supply!

Makes 30

sunflower oil for greasing
30 circles of edible paper, approximately
    7.5cm/3in in diameter
125g/4oz/1 cup blanched almonds
2 egg whites, chilled
400g/14oz/3½ cups icing (confectioners')
    sugar
½ teaspoon ground cinnamon
oil for greasing

Pre-heat the oven to 160°C/325°F/Gas Mark 3. Very lightly oil 2 or 3 baking sheets and arrange the circles of edible paper on the sheets in neat rows without touching. Set aside.

Put the almonds on another baking sheet and put them in the oven for about 5 minutes to toast lightly. Chop them finely in the food processor. Raise the temperature of the oven to 180°C/350°F/Gas Mark 4.

Beat the egg whites until very stiff, then fold in the chopped almonds. Gradually sift in three-quarters of the icing (confectioners') sugar and the cinnamon.

Spoon this meringue mixture on to the circles. Bake for about 15 minutes, or until just firm. Cool on wire racks and trim off any paper which might appear around the edges of the pastry. Dust with the remaining icing sugar and serve at room temperature.

Calabria

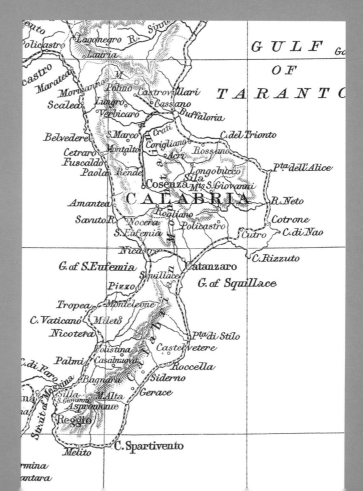

Calabria

Calabria is at the very tip of Italy, a sharp toe which juts out arrogantly into the straits of Messina. Standing on the quayside in Reggio Calabria, you can watch the lights of Sicily twinkling across the water, a mere three kilometres away. The Calabrians, however, are quick to point out that although their accent, their looks and their general attitude might remind you of the Sicilians, they are quite definitely *not* part of Sicily.

This is a mysterious region, with hidden traditions and customs that are impossible to understand but in a strange sort of way add to Calabria's enigmatic appeal. In the course of my various visits to the south, I must confess that this is the one region where I have actually felt a little nervous about travelling on my own. I sense a harshness in the air here, a sort of angry undercurrent.

The local religious ceremonies seem to be filled with a kind of furious anguish that has little to do with gentle Christian goodness. Many Calabrians still periodically indulge in the practice of hauling enormously heavy, ten metre high statues of Madonnas or other patron saints on their shoulders, preferably in bare feet, over several kilometres in the baking sun, as a sign of their immense devotion and sacrifice. They are fervently religious, and fanatically traditional, and have a reputation for stubbornness that is symbolized by the following local fable:

One day a peasant was on his way to Rome when a man (who was actually God) stopped him and asked him where he was going.

'To Rome,' answered the peasant.

'Don't you mean to Rome, God willing?' asked the stranger.

'I am going to Rome even if God is not willing,' answered the stubborn peasant. No sooner were the words out of his mouth, than he was turned into a frog in a nearby marsh.

Later, when God felt like it, he turned the peasant back into a human. Without even pausing, the peasant continued on his way to Rome as though nothing had happened. After a while, God appeared beside the peasant again and asked, 'Where are you going?'

'To Rome,' the peasant replied, as before.

'Don't you mean, to Rome, God willing?' asked God.

'Well, if God doesn't will, there is the marsh,' answered the peasant without breaking his step. This time, God merely smiled at his obstinacy, and left the peasant to walk on in peace.

Calabria was first colonized by the Bruzian tribes, approximately until the eighth century BC, when the area became part of Magna Graecia, and the Greeks named it Bretia. Between the eighth and the fifth century BC there was large-scale Greek colonization of southern Italy. Most of those who came to the toe of Italy were colonists from the northern Peloponnese. Locri, Reggio Calabria, Capo Colonna and Sibari are all sites of ancient Greek cities and bear testimony to the part which Calabria played in the cultural explosion which took place in the New Greece.

We still describe the height of luxurious living as sybaritic, and it is from the ancient town of Sibari, famous for its decadence and outrageous excesses, that this word derives. Sadly, very little remains of the city of high living, destroyed in 510 BC by the inhabitants of a neighbouring town, who diverted a river in order to flood the place out, and presumably to wash away its sinful behaviour! In 444 BC, Hippodamus, the man who designed Piraeus, built the city of Thurii on the same site.

One of the founders of this new city was the writer Herodotus, widely considered to be Europe's very first historian. An extremely well travelled man, he ventured as far afield as southern Russia, the Balkans and the Middle East and has left us detailed accounts of his findings.

At Capo Colonna you can see the ruins of a temple dating from the sixth century BC, dedicated to Hera, although sadly much of it has been allowed to deteriorate in the last three centuries. Further south, at Locri, are the ruins of the sacred Temple of Aphrodite, whose history offers an excellent example of the kind of life which the Greeks enjoyed throughout their colony: the priests of the temple were special pimps who were in control of the many temple prostitutes. For a small fee, pilgrims who made the journey to Locri could pay homage to the goddess in a literal and enjoyable way!

Reggio Calabria, now the regional capital, was once a major Greek city. Very little remains of this except for parts of the ancient city walls. However, the Bronzi di Riace, two spectacular bronze statues found on the sea bed at Riace and thought to be the work of Pheidas, who designed the Elgin Marbles, are among the exhibits on view in the excellent museum.

Rome fought hard, long campaigns all over the south against Pyrrhus and Hannibal, and after the Second Punic War, Calabria eventually came under Roman rule. During the second century BC various Roman settlements were founded along the Capua–Reggio road.

Under the Romans, Calabria plummeted from the glorious dizzy heights of Magna Graecia to bitter misery and hardship, briefly alleviated by the rule of Theodoricus from AD 494 to 526. But the joy that the region had once experienced was never to be repeated, and the misery continued most vividly until the end of the Roman Empire, when the region was passed back and forth between Byzantium and the Longobards. Periods of split and shifting loyalties followed for many long, hard years, until unity was resumed under Byzantine rule in the tenth century. For the next hundred years, however, the region was subjected to violent Saracen attacks, which destabilized Calabria completely until the eleventh century, when Norman rule brought some order to the region.

This lasted until the twelfth century, when Calabria joined the rest of southern Italy in a long and desperate period of chaotic change. The Hohenstaufen, Angevins and Aragons all took over and ruled in turn, but none of them gave Calabria any stability or economic power. In 1815, the former Bourbon king Joachim Murat landed at Pizzo in the hope of finding willing followers to help him regain his throne, but by now the Calabrians had had enough. Five days later, having found no support, he was executed.

Many claim that the high incidence of adult

illiteracy in Calabria (and much of the south) is largely due to the appalling lack of care and intelligence shown by the succession of foreign kings. Under the stupid and weak Ferdinand II, Calabria's oppression reached unbearable levels.

When Garibaldi finally made his surprise landing at Melito, near Reggio Calabria, in 1860, guerrilla bands had already been at work throughout the Calabrian mountains. Dissatisfaction, anger and despair were all very close to the surface. Garibaldi found ten thousand men and women ready to follow him. They had no shoes, no proper weapons and very little food, but they were driven by their sense of frustration and despair; they were battle hardened and ready for anything. It is said that Italy's unification was won with intellect in the north, and with frustrated passion in the south. Calabria has won a heroic position in Italian history that few have ever forgotten.

Since the unification, Calabria has continued to struggle against the various problems which beset it. The ever-changing landscape of mountain and coast is constantly threatened by earthquakes, landslides and flooding. The region has been so desperately neglected for so long that huge amounts of money are required to help it develop. The three provinces of Catanzaro, Cosenza and Reggio di Calabria tend to exist largely in isolation from one another, so that the region lacks a sense of unity and strength. An extended, updated motorway system would help to bring the region together, as would the development of the few industrial installations. These would provide employment, and help to stem the great tide of emigrants who travel north to find work.

Yet despite all the problems, Calabria's violent history and her religious fanatacism have given her people an amazingly resilient quality, which has kept the region and her customs very much alive.

Nowhere is Calabria's resilience and passion more obvious than in the food which is enjoyed here. For many years, Calabrians have had a reputation for cooking food which is extremely heavy and lacking in finesse, and I have to agree that many of their more traditional dishes tend to be very hearty indeed! Fortunately, however, there is a group of fervent new generation Calabrian cooks who are cooking some of the traditional dishes in a much more modern style. The result is an emerging cuisine which makes the most of all the traditional ingredients such as chilli, pork, tomatoes and olive oil in dishes which are light, fresh and appealing.

In the unassuming little town of Castrovillari I found a restaurant which specialised in taking the old recipes of the region and fine tuning them into stunningly modern creations. I ate a dish there which was apparently created in the sixteenth century, using medallions of pork fillet cooked in honey and chilli: absolutely delicious! Further south in Cosenza, I had my first taste of Swordfish Carpaccio – airmail paper thin sheets of fresh swordfish, sprinkled with lemon juice, olive oil and salt and pepper and left to marinate before serving, lightly chilled.

The traditional cooking of Calabria is the kind of food suited to people who are used to working very hard. From the much loved and respected pig come a wide range of pork dishes, the most important of which are the vast range of different kinds of sausages and salame produced for the express purpose of seeing households through the snowy winter months, high on the densely wooded slopes of the Sila mountain. The women of Calabria have long been famous for the countless pasta shapes they are capable of fashioning from a simple flour and water dough. These are then combined with fish, vegetables, tomato sauces, chilli sauces or, more rarely, meat sauces to make entire wholesome meals.

On the slopes of the Sila, or tucked away in the inland villages, you'll come across Calabria's famous range of cheeses – buttirro, rinusu, tuma, impanata, all of them tasting of sun-warmed grasslands and ice-cold winter frosts. Vegetables and pulses are stewed either separately or together, or added to pasta to make deliciously satisfying dishes, and there is a vast range of salads to enjoy during the scorching hot summer months.

All the traditional dishes of Calabria tend to have a certain degree of austerity about them. Simple cooking methods such as the spit, skillet or grill are very much in evidence, with very few recipes that can be considered sophisticated or complicated. That is not to say there is any shortage of excellent produce: superb vegetables preserved in olive oil; huge, juicy vegetables such as peppers, tomatoes, courgettes and aubergines; the wide range of delicious cheeses; rich and fruity olive oil, marvellous pasta and cured meats and all kinds of fresh fish as well as the ubiquitous swordfish.

But it is with the pastries and cakes that the Calabrian flair and imagination comes into its own. Many of these specialities are actually the work of nuns who have traditionally created them within the walls of their convents for holy festivities such as the day of the local patron saint, or other days of special religious significance. Others are simple home-made biscuits or pastries made for special occasions by the women of the family, using the most basic of ingredients but shaping them to appear as exciting and imaginative as possible.

Finally, a word about the wines of Calabria. First of all, the intense heat makes these wines extremely strong and very alcoholic. There are three that I consider to be of special note: Savuto, also known as *Succo di Pietra* (juice of the rock), is a very dry, bright red wine with a velvety finish – perfect with rich meat dishes or game. Ciro is the wine which was drunk by the very first Olympian athletes in order to give them strength and power for the Games. It has a ruby red or deep pink colour, with a very fragrant nose, and is delicious with grilled meat or game. The white version is very smooth tasting, straw yellow in colour, and very good with any fish dish with a sauce. Greco di Gerace is one of the oldest wines in all of Italy. The grapes used to make this golden wine, with its intense perfume of orange blossom and beautifully rounded, velvety flavour, come from vinestocks originally imported to Calabria from the Peloponnese in the eighth century BC. The wine is still made in the time-honoured way – by drying the grapes out slightly in the sun after picking and before pressing.

Melanzane Sott'olio

Aubergines Preserved in Olive Oil

All kinds of vegetables preserved in olive oil often form a part of the antipasto course in Italian meals. They are delicious with, for example, slices of salami and plenty of crusty bread. There are so many recipes for this very popular local speciality, because aubergines (eggplants), like peppers, courgettes (zucchini), chillies and tomatoes, are the vegetables which epitomize the southern regions. Traditionally, a big, smooth round river or seabed rock is used as a weight, and the receptacle used to keep the aubergines in is called a *salaturi*, which is a tall terracotta pot with a glazed interior and a lid.

Makes about 10kg/21 lb

10kg/20lb aubergines (eggplants), peeled
    and cut into 0.5cm/¼in slices
350g/12oz/1½ cups coarse sea salt
8–9 dried red chilli peppers
10 cloves garlic, peeled and sliced into
    quarters
2 teaspoons dried oregano
1 litre/1¾ pints/4½ cups olive oil

Place the aubergines (eggplants) all in a large bowl in layers, covering each layer with salt. When they are all in the bowl, place a cover over them and then lay a heavy weight on top. Incline the bowl slightly to let the juice run out. Leave like this, in a cool place, for 12 hours, occasionally tipping out the juice.

Rinse briefly and squeeze each aubergine slice as dry as possible. Begin to arrange them in a tall preserving jar, preferably a *salaturi*, in layers, scattering garlic, chilli and dried oregano between each layer as you go along. Press each layer down very tightly to prevent air becoming trapped between the aubergines. When the jars are full to the brim, place a heavy weight on top. Leave like this for about 1 month.

Remove the weight and pour in enough olive oil to cover them completely and refill the jar. Leave the aubergines to mature for a further 20 days before eating.

Pomodori Secchi Sott'olio

Sun-dried Tomatoes Preserved in Olive Oil

It goes without saying that there are two absolutely vital ingredients for this dish, which are hard to come by in countries where the weather is not scorchingly hot! You need sweet, scented, luscious tomatoes and pounding, scorching sunshine, both of which are widely available in Calabria!

Makes about 10kg/21lb

10kg/20lb fresh, ripe firm tomatoes
1 litre/1¾ pints/4½ cups red wine vinegar
    mixed with 500ml/¾ pint/2 cups cold
    water
9 cloves garlic, finely chopped
3 teaspoons dried oregano
8 dried red chilli peppers, finely chopped
5 sticks celery with leaves if possible, finely
    chopped
150g/5oz fresh basil leaves, finely
    shredded with your hands
125g/4oz/⅔ cup salted capers, well
    rinsed, dried and finely chopped
salt
about 2 litres/3½ pints/9 cups olive oil

Cut all the tomatoes in half, remove as many of the seeds as you can and lay them side by side on planks of wood in direct sunlight for 5–6 days. They are ready only when every last drop of juice has evaporated from them and they are shrivelled and almost brittle. Rinse the tomatoes in the vinegar and water mixture, then leave them to dry out while you prepare the dressing.

Mix together the garlic, oregano, chilli, celery, basil and capers. Arrange the tomatoes in layers in a preserving jar, scattering some of this mixture over each layer. Season with a little salt as you create each layer.

Press each layer down very firmly with your hands to squeeze out any air which might become trapped between the layers. When the jar is about three-quarters full, pour in enough oil to fill the jar to the brim. Cover and leave to mature for about 5 months before eating.

Mille Cosedde

A Thousand Things

The name of this soup does not, of course, mean that there are really 1,000 different ingredients, but simply that there are many different things in it! It is a Calabrian version of the classical Minestrone, with various different pulses and mushrooms.

Serves 4–6

200g/7oz/1½ cups dried broad (fava) beans
200g/7oz/1 cup dried borlotti beans
100g/3½oz/1 cup chick-peas
100g/3½oz/½ cup brown lentils
1 Savoy cabbage, rinsed and trimmed
250g/8oz full-flavoured fresh mushrooms, wiped
125g/4oz/1 cup pancetta, chopped
1 large carrot, peeled and chopped
1 large onion, peeled and chopped
4 cloves garlic, chopped
3 tablespoons olive oil
salt and freshly milled black pepper
2 litres/3½ pints/9 cups boiling water
200g/7oz small, tubular-shaped pasta
125g/4oz/1 cup pecorino cheese, grated

Soak all the pulses separately for one night. Drain and rinse them, then put them into 4 different saucepans with fresh water and boil each for 5 minutes. Drain each one again, then return them separately to their saucepans with further fresh water. Bring to the boil, then simmer until tender. When each one is soft and tender (they will cook at different times), drain and set aside.

Boil or steam the cabbage until tender, then shred it finely and set aside. Cook the mushrooms in a little water until just soft, then slice them thickly and set aside.

Fry the pancetta, in a large saucepan with the carrot, onion and garlic until the vegetables are soft. Add the mushrooms and season with salt and pepper. Pour in the boiling water and stir together thoroughly.

As soon as the soup begins to boil, add the cabbage. Stir and return to the boil, then add all the pulses. Return to the boil again, then simmer for about 10 minutes. Add the pasta, stir and simmer until the pasta is just tender. Adjust the seasoning to taste and serve with the pecorino offered separately.

Minestra di Cavolo
Cabbage Soup

The simplest cabbage soup I have ever come across! This recipe proves that as long as you use top-quality ingredients – in this case best beef stock and excellent, fresh, crisp, flavourful cabbage – you need very little else!

Serves 4

1 fresh, Savoy cabbage, trimmed, cored and
  very finely shredded
salt
2.5 litres/4½ pints/11¼ cups best beef
  stock
125g/4oz/1 cup freshly grated pecorino
  cheese
8 thin slices ciabatta bread, toasted

Cover the cabbage in cold, salted water, bring to the boil and boil for about 5 minutes. Drain and set aside.

Bring the stock to a slow boil, toss in the cabbage and boil again for about 10 minutes. Serve at once, offering the cheese and toasted ciabatta separately.

Polenta Verde
Green Polenta

In other southern regions, apart from Lazio, polenta hardly features at all. But in the Sila mountains the winters get very cold indeed, and there is nothing more warming than a dish of rib-sticking polenta. The nearby lakes and rivers provide sufficient water to grow at least some maize (corn), from which the golden yellow polenta flour is produced. With inevitable Calabrian flair and style, cooks here have managed to create something relatively exotic out of the simplest of ingredients: maize flour (corn meal), water, dripping and broccoli. Calabrian proverb: 'If you want your polenta to taste good, only add the flour when the water is singing.'

Serves 4–6

salt
500g/1lb tender, leafy broccoli florets
  (flowerets)
500g/1lb/3 cups polenta flour
125g/4oz pancetta or guanciale, very finely
  chopped and mixed into 125g/4oz/½
  cup pork dripping
¼ teaspoon freshly milled black pepper or
  crushed chillies
¼ teaspoon fennel seeds, crushed lightly

Bring 3 litres/5¼ pints/13 cups water to the boil with 2 pinches of salt. Toss in the broccoli and boil for about 3 minutes.

Polenta Verde / Green Polenta

Trickle in the polenta flour very slowly, beating constantly to avoid any lumps. Simmer for about 30 minutes, stirring constantly with a wooden spoon, then stir in the pancetta and dripping and cook for a further 10 minutes, stirring. Season with salt, the pepper and the fennel seeds. Cook for a further 10 minutes, or until the polenta comes away cleanly from the sides of the pot, stirring. Tip it out on to a wooden board and leave to cool for about 4 minutes. Serve in large slabs alongside a selection of cheeses.

Maccheroncelli Ammuddicati

Maccheroncelli with Breadcrumbs

In Southern Italy, breadcrumbs are often used instead of grated cheese on pasta, either because there is simply no cheese available, or no money with which to buy any. You will find recipes using breadcrumbs in this way all over the south.

Serves 4

4 tablespoons olive oil
3 cloves garlic, chopped
250g/8oz fresh, ripe tomatoes, quartered and seeded
10 leaves fresh basil, torn into shreds
salt
125g/4oz/1 cup dried coarse breadcrumbs
2–3 tablespoons grated Parmesan cheese
4 tablespoons chopped fresh parsley
500g/1lb maccheroncelli, or any small tubular shaped pasta

Heat the oil in a large pan and fry the garlic, until the garlic is transparent. Add the tomatoes and the basil and season with salt. Stir well and cover. Leave to simmer, adding water if necessary, for about 30 minutes on a relatively high heat. Bring a large pan of salted water to a rolling boil for the pasta.

Meanwhile, mix together the breadcrumbs with the cheese and parsley. When the tomato sauce is ready, toss the pasta into the boiling water. Stir, return to the boil and cook until just tender. Drain well and return to the pan.

Pour over the tomato sauce and toss together. Divide it between 4 soup plates, sprinkle each portion generously with the breadcrumb mixture and serve at once.

Pasta chi Cucuzzeddi

Pasta with Courgettes

I particularly like this version of this Calabrian speciality because it relies almost completely on the inimitable flavour of the courgettes (zucchini), which in this area are always packed with flavour and deliciously perfumed.

Serves 4

500g/1lb tender courgettes (zucchini), topped and tailed and sliced
12 tablespoons olive oil
5 cloves garlic, coarsely chopped
400g/14oz vermicelli
125g/4oz/2 cups fresh basil, torn into shreds
125g/4oz/1 cup hard, salted grated ricotta cheese, or freshly grated, mature Parmesan cheese

Fry the courgettes (zucchini) in the olive oil until golden. Drain on kitchen paper (paper towels) and fry the garlic in the same olive oil. Set aside until required, off the heat.

Bring a large pan of salted water to a rolling boil. Toss in the vermicelli, stir, return to the boil and cook until just tender. Drain well and return to the pan containing the oil and garlic. Toss together quickly over a medium heat, add the courgettes and basil and toss again.

Heat through thoroughly, then transfer to a warmed serving platter and serve with the cheese offered separately.

Minestra di Fave e Cardi

Broad Bean and Cardoon Soup

You can use fresh, frozen or dried broad (fava) beans for this dish. If you use dried beans, you must remember to soak them and pre-boil them as normal (pages 50-1). To my mind, nothing quite beats the flavour of fresh vegetables!

Serves 4

500g/1lb fresh broad (fava) beans, shelled
salt and freshly milled black pepper
1 onion, peeled and chopped
3 tablespoons olive oil
1kg/2lb cardoons, trimmed, strung, rinsed
 and cut into mathsticks
600ml/1 pint/2½ cups beef stock

Cover the beans with cold, salted water, bring to the boil and boil until completely tender. Push through a sieve (strainer) without draining.

Fry the onion in the olive oil until soft, then stir in the broad (fava) bean purée and season to taste with salt and pepper. Simmer for 5–10 minutes, then add about half the stock and the cardoons. Stir and simmer until the cardoons are completely cooked, only adding more stock if necessary. This soup is supposed to be fairly thick. Serve hot or cold but not chilled.

Braciolette di Pesce Spada

Swordfish Steaks

In Calabria, swordfish is much more than just an ingredient, it is a way of life. The glorious silver fish, which for as long as anyone can remember have scythed their way through the currents of the Messina Straits, are somehow an ideal representation of the strong macho image of this region: a perfect mixture of grace and power. The ancient killing ritual called 'La Mattanza', which was an integral part of the hunt, has almost completely disappeared these days, although there was a time when the men who set out on their boats to stab the fish (helplessly trapped in the nets) would turn the water red with blood for miles around. Nowadays, somewhat more humane methods of catching these beautiful animals are practised almost everywhere in the south.

Serves 4

125g/4oz/2 cups fine fresh breadcrumbs
50g/2oz/½ cup freshly grated pecorino
    cheese
4 cloves garlic, finely chopped
3 tablespoons salted capers, rinsed, dried
    and finely chopped
9 tablespoons olive oil
salt and freshly milled black pepper
8 thin, small slices swordfish, total weight
    about 1.2kg/2lb 6oz
2 lemons, finely sliced, to garnish

Mix the breadcrumbs with the cheese, garlic and capers. Moisten with about 3 tablespoons of the oil and season with salt and pepper.

Brush the fish steaks on both sides with olive oil. Spread the breadcrumb paste all over the fish on both sides. Brush with the remaining oil. Roll the fish steaks up on themselves and secure them closed with wooden cocktail sticks (toothpicks).

Grill (broil) on all sides for about 10 minutes, turning the fish rolls over frequently. Serve on a warmed platter, garnished with the sliced lemons.

Zuppa di Baccalà alla Calabrese

Salt Cod Stew with Red Peppers and Potatoes

When you buy *stoccafisso* or *baccalà* it always looks unbelievably unappetizing. I once mentioned this to a Calabrian friend who told me gravely that the more it looks like a dirty old dishcloth, the better it will taste once cooked. Considering how much fresh fish and seafood is available round the region, I was surprised to see just how popular dried cod and salted herring actually are – they even salt and dry tuna in certain areas! Make sure you really soak and reconstitute the fish thoroughly before starting to prepare the dish.

Serves 4

1kg/2lb dried salt cod (*baccalà*), soaked in
    several changes of cold water over 3 days
500g/1lb fist-sized potatoes, peeled and
    halved
6 tablespoons olive oil
¼ teaspoon crushed red chilli pepper
4 juicy, large red peppers, cored, seeded
    and chopped

Clean, bone, skin and trim the fish very carefully. Cut it into large chunks and arrange it in a flameproof casserole. Add the potatoes, drizzle with a little olive oil and, sprinkle with chilli pepper and add the peppers. Drizzle with the remaining oil and then add enough water to barely cover the fish and potatoes.

Cover and simmer gently for 1-2 hours, or until the fish flakes and the potatoes are completely soft. Serve piping hot.

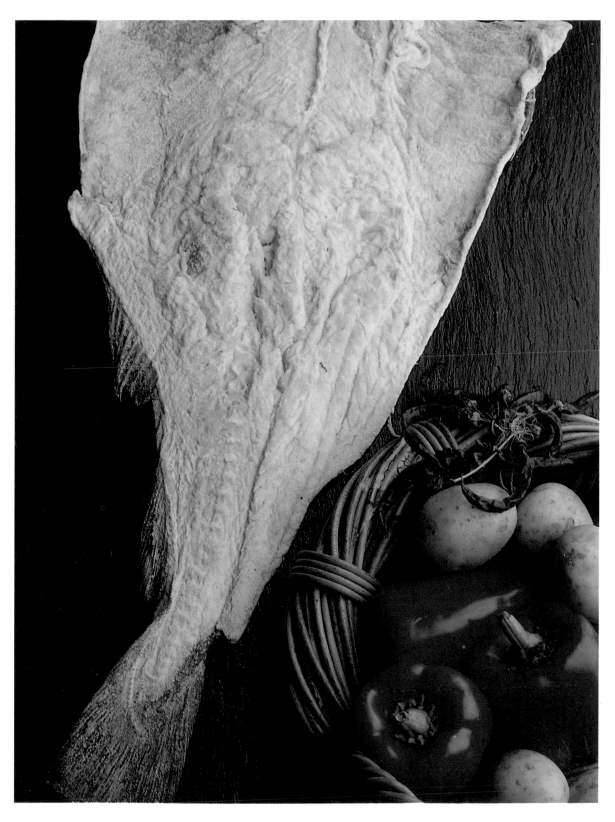

Zuppa di Baccalà alla Calabrese/Salt Cod Stew with
Red Peppers and Potatoes

Tonno alla Calabrese

Fresh Tuna Casserole

Tuna is probably the second most important fish to be consumed in the region, though it does not appear to have any of the impressive chauvinistic connotations which are associated with the swordfish! Fresh tuna is completely different from the canned variety, especially if it is freshly caught. This delicious recipe has become an Italian classic.

Serves 4

800g/¾lb fresh tuna (in 4 even-sized
   steaks)
1 large clove garlic, peeled
1 onion, peeled
salt and freshly milled black pepper
4 tablespoons olive oil
2 tablespoons plain white (all-purpose)
   flour
4 tablespoons dry white wine
50g/2oz/½ cup pancetta, finely chopped
2 tablespoons chopped fresh parsley
4 anchovy fillets preserved in oil, drained,
   boned and patted dry
300g/10oz/1½ cups canned tomatoes,
   drained, seeded and chopped
½ hot dried red chilli pepper, chopped

Wash the tuna in cold water and pat it dry. Chop the garlic and onion together and set aside. Season the dry tuna steaks thoroughly on both sides with salt and pepper.

Heat the oil in a wide frying pan (skillet). Coat the tuna lightly on either side in flour, then quickly fry the steaks for 3 minutes on both sides in the hot oil. Sprinkle with the wine and allow the alcohol to boil off for 1 minute. Remove the fish and drain well on kitchen paper (paper towels). Fry the pancetta, garlic and onion and half the parsley in the oil for about 5 minutes, stirring, then add the anchovy fillets and mash them into the hot oil with a fork. After a minute or so, add the tomatoes and stir together thoroughly. Add the chilli and simmer slowly for about 15 minutes.

Slide in the fish and heat through thoroughly for about 8 minutes, turning the fish steaks over gently once. Arrange the tuna on a warmed serving dish, cover with the sauce and sprinkle with the remaining parsley just before serving.

Costa di Maiale alla Silana

Pork Ribs with Tomatoes, Mushrooms and Artichokes

Preserved artichoke hearts and preserved mushrooms are used in this recipe, giving a very unusual flavour to the whole dish. Only in Calabria are preserved vegetables used so frequently in the preparation of hot dishes. This is an ideal recipe for a barbecue, as the ribs taste much better if cooked outdoors.

Serves 4

300g/10oz/1½ cups canned tomatoes, drained, seeded and coarsely chopped
4–5 tablespoons olive oil
salt and freshly milled black pepper
12 fresh basil leaves, coarsely shredded
50g/2oz/⅔ cup mushrooms preserved in olive oil, finely chopped
50g/2oz/½ cup artichoke hearts preserved in olive oil, finely chopped
1 dessertspoon pork dripping
8 pork rib chops

Fry the tomatoes in the oil in a saucepan for about 15 minutes. Season with salt and freshly milled black pepper, add the basil leaves and simmer for a further 15 minutes. Add the mushrooms and artichoke hearts with their oil to the tomato sauce. Stir together thoroughly, then add the dripping and continue simmering for a further 10 minutes.

Grill (broil) or barbecue the rib chops and serve with the sauce offered separately.

Tortiera di Carciofi

Savoury Artichoke Cake

Another marvellous dish to take on a picnic. The artichoke, too, has a place among the many vegetables that local cooks hold so dear and use in a thousand and one different recipes. This is normally served as a main course.

Serves 6

8 tablespoons olive oil
4 globe artichokes
1 lemon, cut in half
juice of ½ lemon
8 tablespoons fresh white breadcrumbs
3 tablespoons chopped fresh parsley
2 cloves garlic, very finely chopped
salt
50g/2oz/½ cup freshly grated pecorino cheese
4 medium to large potatoes, peeled and cut into 2cm/¾in slices
50g/2oz/⅓ cup capers, rinsed, dried and coarsely chopped

Prepare the artichokes very carefully. Cut away the artichoke stalk (stem). Remove all the hard exterior leaves with a sharp knife. Cut off all the sharp tips with a pair of scissors. Cut it in half and cut out the hairy choke. Rub it all over with the cut lemon. Slice it in half again and then slice each quarter into three segments. Snip any sharp ends off with scissors. Drop the cut artichokes into a bowl of water with the lemon juice. Repeat with the remaining artichokes and leave them to soak for 30 minutes.

Meanwhile, preheat the oven to 160°C/325°F/ Gas Mark 3. Grease a deep 20cm/8in cake tin (pan) with 1 tablespoon of olive oil. Mix together

6 tablespoons of the breadcrumbs, the parsley, garlic, pecorino, a pinch of salt and about I tablespoon of the olive oil.

Scatter the remaining plain breadcrumbs all over the sides and the bottom of the cake tin. Arrange a layer of potato across the bottom. Drain and dry the artichokes.

Sprinkle the potatoes with some of the capers and some of the breadcrumb mixture, then cover with a layer of artichokes. Sprinkle with a little oil and repeat these layers again until you have used up all the ingredients. Make sure you save some oil to drizzle over the top.

Press down with your hand to compress the layers. Cover with a tight lid or heavy ovenproof plate to keep all the layers tightly compressed. Bake for about 50 minutes, then turn the tin upside down so the lid is on the bottom. Lower the oven to 140°C/275°F/Gas Mark I and bake for a further 30 minutes. Take out of the oven and leave to stand for about 10 minutes before tipping the 'cake' out on to a serving platter. Serve hot with various salads.

Scarola Ripiena

Stuffed Escarole

The escarole is a variety of salad green with wide, dark green curly leaves. The plant is often blanched by the earth surrounding it or it is sometimes grown in cellars. In this recipe, the whole lettuces are dropped into boiling stock and cooked until tender before being served either as a soup or as a main course.

Serves 4

salt and freshly milled black pepper
4 escarole heads, trimmed and well rinsed
500g/Ilb minced (ground) beef
2 stale bread rolls, covered in cold water to soak for 20 minutes, then coarsely crumbled
I egg, beaten
7 tablespoons freshly grated Parmesan cheese
1.2 litres/2½ pints/6¼ cups beef or chicken stock

Bring a large pan of salted water to the boil. Toss in the escarole, return to the boil and boil for about 5 minutes. Drain and dry well inside and out.

Mix together the minced (ground) beef, bread, egg and cheese. Season with salt and pepper. Use this filling to stuff the centre of each lettuce head. Take out a couple of the central leaves to make room and then tie the lettuces closed with string.

Bring the stock to the boil, drop the stuffed lettuce heads into the stock and boil for about 20 minutes. Serve at once.

Melanzane alla Finitese

Fried Aubergines with Pecorino Cheese

Here is a very filling dish with plenty of punchy flavours. Boiling the aubergines (eggplants) first means they need to spend less time frying and end up being less greasy and heavy on the digestion.

Melanzane alla Finitese / Fried Aubergines with Pecorino Cheese

Serves 4

salt

4 aubergines (eggplants), tops cut off and
  cut into 1cm/½in thick slices

150g/5oz/1¼ cups pecorino cheese,
  coarsely grated

about 25 leaves fresh basil, torn into small
  shreds

1 small red chilli, finely chopped

1 clove garlic, finely chopped

¼ teaspoon salt

4 tablespoons plain white (all-purpose)
  flour, sifted

1 litre/1¾ pints/4½ cups sunflower oil

Bring a pan of salted water to the boil. Toss in the
aubergine (eggplant) slices and boil for about 3
minutes, then drain and pat dry with kichen paper
(paper towels).

Make sandwiches between slices of aubergine,
dividing the cheese, basil, chilli and garlic and salt
evenly between all the aubergines. Secure them all
closed with wooden cocktail sticks (toothpicks)
and then coat each sandwich lightly in flour.

Heat the oil until a small piece of bread
dropped into the oil sizzles instantly. Fry each
sandwich in the hot oil until golden brown. Drain
well on kitchen paper (paper towels) and serve hot.

Purgatorio alla Calabrese
Calabrian Purgatory

This is unquestionably one of my favourite recipes
from this region. The vegetables that grow here are
so sweet, highly perfumed and juicy that they only
need the simplest of cooking methods to make
them practically sing. In this recipe, after stewing
together and scenting with basil, the vegetables are
cosily tucked into a huge round loaf of coarse
country bread: pane casareccio. If you cannot get
hold of this kind of bread, use two or three loaves
of ciabatta or some other kind of Italian bread.
This is the ultimate food for a picnic in the
Calabrian mountains!

Serves 6 to 8

2 aubergines (eggplants), cut into chunks

salt

9 tablespoons olive oil

250g/7oz/1¼ cups fresh tomatoes,
  peeled, seeded and chopped

10 leaves fresh basil

4 peppers, cored, seeded and cut into
  chunks

4 medium-sized new potatoes, scraped and
  cut into the same size as the aubergines
  and peppers

1 large loaf of *pane casareccio*, or 2 loaves of
  ciabatta bread

Sprinkle the aubergines generously with salt and
leave them to stand in a colander, under a weight,
in the sink for about 1 hour. Rinse and dry them
thoroughly.

Heat 3 tablespoons of the oil in a large frying
pan (skillet) and add the tomatoes and the basil.
Season with salt and simmer together for about
15 minutes, covered.

In a separate pan, heat 3 tablespoons of the oil and then season, fry all the other vegetables together, covered, until soft. Tip the vegetables into the tomato sauce and mix together.

Split the bread open and drizzle the inside with the remaining oil, then spread the vegetables and sauce over the bread. Close it like a sandwich and press down lightly. Slice into chunky wedges and serve at once, or wrap and carry to your picnic!

Fagioli d'Estate

Summer beans

For this recipe you really do need to use fresh borlotti beans in their pods. In Italy, fresh beans are widely available during the summer months, hence the name of this dish. Tradition dictates you should leave half the beans in their pods, but this only applies to really tender young pods. If your fresh beans are the older, coarser variety, then shell them all.

Serves 4

1 large red onion, peeled and sliced
5 tablespoons olive oil
125g/4oz/½ cup ripe fresh tomatoes, peeled, seeded and coarsely chopped
500g/1lb fresh borlotti beans (about half of them shelled, leaving the more tender beans in their pods)
8 leaves fresh basil
3–4 sprigs fresh parsley
salt
125g/4oz ditali pasta, or other short stubby pasta shape

Fry the onion slowly in the oil until soft and golden. Stir in the tomatoes and fry gently for about 5 minutes.

Add all the beans, shelled or not, stir, cover and simmer for about 10 minutes, stirring frequently. Cover generously with cold water and bring to the boil, then cover and simmer until the beans are completely soft, adding more hot water as required to keep everything fairly liquid. When the beans are cooked, add the pasta and boil until tender. Cool to room temperature and serve.

Insalata Calabrese

Calabrian Salad

The most important thing about this salad is that the onions used must be as sweet as possible. Onions grown in Tropea are naturally sweeter and more full of flavour than those grown almost anywhere. In the absence of Tropean onions, you can soak red onions in cold water for half an hour to sweeten their flavour even further.

Serves 4

4 fist-sized potatoes, well scrubbed
salt
8 plum-shaped tomatoes, not over ripe, halved, seeded and sliced
3 red onions, peeled and thinly sliced, then soaked in cold water for 30 minutes
5 leaves fresh basil, torn into shreds
1 heaped teaspoon dried oregano
8 tablespoons olive oil

Cover the potatoes in cold salted water and boil until tender. Drain well and set aside until just cool enough to handle, then peel and slice thinly.

Add the tomatoes to the potatoes. Drain the onions carefully, pat them dry in kitchen towels (paper towels) and add them to the potatoes and tomatoes. Add the basil, oregano, olive oil and a little salt. Toss everything together so it is well mixed and serve at once.

Insalata Arriganata
Potato and Olive Salad

Try this for a very different kind of potato salad! It is perfect with cold meats or cheese, or with cold fish dishes.

Serves 4 to 6

8–10 potatoes, well scrubbed
salt
50g/2oz/⅓ cup black (ripe) olives, stoned (pitted) and sliced in half
20 leaves fresh mint, chopped
3 tablespoons salted capers, well rinsed, dried and chopped
6 cloves garlic, chopped
12 tablespoons olive oil
1 tablespoon dried oregano

Boil the potatoes in salted water until tender. Drain, cool slightly and then slice them.

Place the potato slices in a salad bowl. Sprinkle with the chopped olives, mint, capers, garlic, oil and oregano. Mix everything together, taste to check for seasoning and leave to stand for about 10 minutes. Toss once again and serve.

Zucca Gialla alla Calabrese
Yellow Pumpkin with Mint and Capers

This dish tastes as strange as it sounds when you read through it, although it is not at all unpleasant – merely slightly odd! Fairly punchy in flavour, it make a good cold accompaniment for cold meat, especially pork.

Serves 4-6

750g/1½lb orange or yellow pumpkin, peeled, seeded and sliced with membranes removed
4 tablespoons coarse sea salt
500ml/¾ pint/2 cups sunflower oil
10 tablespoons olive oil
4 tablespoons red wine vinegar
3 tablespoons salted capers, well rinsed, dried and finely chopped
5 cloves garlic, sliced into slivers
5 tablespoons chopped fresh mint
8 tablespoons fine dry breadcrumbs

*Zucca Gialla alla Calabrese/Yellow Pumpkin with
Mint and Capers*

Arrange the pumpkin evenly in a colander, sprinkled with salt. Put a weight on top and leave it to drain for about 1 hour.

Rinse and pat dry the pumpkin slices. Heat the oil until a small piece of bread dropped into it sizzles instantly. Fry the pumpkin for about 4 minutes on both sides, working in batches if necessary, then drain well on kitchen paper (paper towels).

Mix the oil and vinegar with the capers, garlic, mint, and half the breadcrumbs. Arrange half the pumpkin in a layer in a dish and cover with half the dressing. Cover with another layer of pumpkin, then cover with the remaining dressing. Press down firmly with your hands and coat with the remaining breadcrumbs. Leave to stand for 1 hour before serving.

Zeppole a Vento
Honey-coated Fritters

There can be nothing simpler, yet more effective, than to take the simplest and most easily available ingredients and turning them into something that is pretty to look at, and delicious to eat. To my mind, this is the essence of every Italian cook, but it is truer than ever in Calabria, especially when it comes to the vast array of delicate pastries, delicious cakes and crumbly biscuits (cookies), and the fantastic assortment of fried sweets.

Makes about 15 to 20

500g/1lb/heaped 4 cups very fine white plain (cake) flour, sifted twice
about 1 litre/1¾ pints/4½ cups light olive oil for deep-frying
5 tablespoons liquid honey

Bring 500ml/¾ pint/2 cups water to the boil. Gradually trickle in the flour, stirring constantly to prevent lumps until the mixture comes away from the sides of the saucepan. Tip the dough into a bowl and leave to cool completely. Roll it out into cylinders about 5cm/2in long and squeeze them in the middle to make bow shapes.

When they are all made, heat the oil until a small piece of bread dropped into it sizzles instantly. Fry all the bows, working in batches, if necessary, until golden and crisp. Drain well on kitchen paper (paper towels), then arrange on a warmed platter.

Meanwhile, heat the honey until just bubbling, then pour all over the fritters. Cool slightly then serve while still warm.

Torta reggina
Reggio Calabria Cake

This is almost like a fruit pie, although the sweet pastry is very different to the kind usually found in mother's apple pie! A brilliant way to make the most of the fruits of the summer! It is named after the capital city of the region.

Serves 6 to 8

1kg/2lb assorted fresh fruit, such as apples, pears, cherries and plums
300g/10oz/1⅓ cups plain white (all-purpose) flour
2 egg yolks
200g/7oz/14 tablespoons unsalted butter
200g/7oz/1 cup caster (superfine) flour
finely grated rind (peel) of 1 lemon
1 tablespoon lard
1 egg, beaten, for glazing

Peel and core or stone (pit) all the fruit as appropriate. Poach lightly in water until just tender. Drain very thoroughly and set aside.

Pile all the flour on the tabletop and make a hollow in the centre with your fist. Add the egg yolks, butter, half the sugar and the grated lemon rind (peel). Make a very soft pastry (dough), cover and leave to rest for about 20 minutes.

Meanwhile, preheat the oven to 220°C/ 425°F/Gas Mark 7. Grease a shallow 23.5cm/9in cake tin (pan) with the lard. Roll out half the pastry and use it to line the bottom and sides of the cake tin. Do not be too worried about it breaking and cracking, as you can just use your fingers to press it together.

Make sure the fruit is well drained and sprinkle it with the remaining sugar. Put in the tin. Roll out the remaining pastry and cover the fruit with it. Pinch the edges together carefully all the way around and brush with beaten egg. Bake for 40 minutes, until the pastry is golden. Serve hot or at room temperature.

Torrone Gelato

Fake Frozen Nougat

A little skill and expertise is necessary to make this successfully, and you will need a loaf pan or terrine mould. Very, very, sweet, this needs to be served with ice cold dry white wine.

Serves 6

1kg/2lb/8 cups icing (confectioners') sugar, sifted
juice of 1–2 lemons, depending on size and amount of juice they contain
3 drops lemon essence (extract)
3 drops cochineal or red food colouring of your choice
30g/1¼oz/⅓ cup cocoa powder, sifted
2 tablespoons almond oil for greasing
50g/2oz/⅓ cup blanched almonds
300g/10oz/1⅓ cups assorted candied fruit
250g/8oz chocolate

Blend the icing (confectioners') sugar with enough of the lemon juice to make a doughy texture – not too runny and not too hard, just enough to be able to knead it with your hands like pastry (dough). Divide the mixture into 3 equal-sized parts. Knead the lemon essence (extract) into the first part. Knead the cochineal into the second part, and add the cocoa powder to the third.

Line a square 1.5kg/3lb bread pan or several smaller pans with oiled greaseproof (wax) paper or baking parchment. Mix together the almonds and candied fruit and divide this into 3 portions as well. Mix one-third of the nuts and fruit into each of the 3 parts of icing sugar paste. Arrange these 3 mixtures in the mould in layers, pressing each one flat as you spoon it into the mould.

Cover and place a weight on the top so as to compress the whole thing into an even-sized block. Chill in the refrigerator for about 3 days.

Melt the chocolate until liquid. Turn out the mould and cover it all over in chocolate. Chill again until the chocolate sets. Serve in thin slices.

Petrali

Calabrian Sweetmeats

To make this very old-fashioned and traditional sweetmeat, allow 12 hours for the filling to rest and the flavours to develop. It is very simple, yet extremely rich in both flavour and texture.

Many different versions for *petrali* appear all over the region. It is quite likely that they were originally created within the walls of the local convents, where the nuns would busy themselves by preparing great quantities of pastries and sweets to sell to the locals. In some parts of the region these are the traditional Christmas pastry, while in other areas they are used to celebrate St Martin's day and are therefore also called *Pitte di San Martino*.

---

water icing (frosting), to decorate
multi-coloured sugar strands, to decorate

for the filling:
3kg/6lb dried figs, whole
2.5kg/5lb blanched almonds, halved
1.5kg/3lb halved walnuts
I teaspoon ground cinnamon
I teaspoon ground cloves
Ikg/2lb/2¾ cups liquid honey
8 tablespoons sweet dessert wine

for the pastry:
Ikg/2lb/8 cups plain white (all-purpose)
    flour
3 eggs
125g/4oz/½ cup lard, diced
200g/7oz/I cup sugar
5 tablespoons sweet vermouth
I½ teaspoons baking powder
I tablespoon olive oil
extra oil for the baking sheet

Make the filling first. Cut the dried figs into quarters. Mix the figs and nuts together in a sauce pan. Stir in the spices, honey and wine and stir over a low heat, slowly simmering, for about 10 minutes. Leave to stand for 12 hours.

Now make the pastry (dough). Pile all the flour on the worktop and make a hollow in the centre with your fist. Put the egg yolks, lard, sugar, vermouth, baking powder and olive oil into the hollow. Knead it all together until you have a smooth, elastic dough. Do not over-knead it. Leave the pastry to rest for 30 minutes.

Roll out the pastry to a thickness of 0.5cm/¼in. Using a pastry cutter or upturned glass with a diameter of 10–12cm/4–5in, cut the pastry into rounds.

Fill half of each round with the fig and nut mixture, fold over the circle and press closed. Seal the edges carefully by going all the way round with the prongs of a fork. You can also leave the pastries open and make a tiny lattice pattern on top, especially if you make other shapes like hearts, flowers, arrows and so on.

Preheat the oven to 180°C/350°F/Gas Mark 4. Arrange all the *petrali* on oiled baking sheets. Bake for about 30 minutes. Cool on cake racks and then ice (frost) them lightly with a plain white water icing (frosting), made by mixing cold water and icing sugar to the texture of thick yoghurt and sprinkle with multi-coloured sugar strands.

Sicily

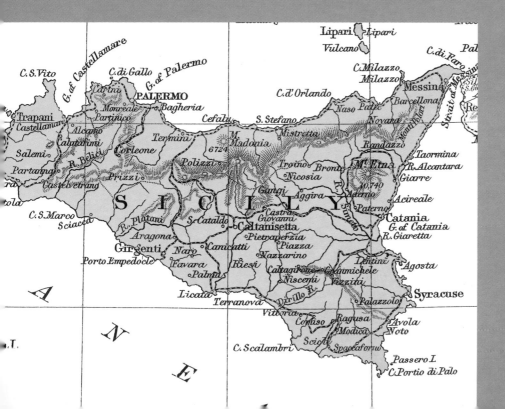

Sicily

The cuisine of Sicily can boast many specialities which are absolutely unique to the island. It is probably the oldest cuisine of the whole country, it is one of the richest and most varied, and is without doubt the most visually spectacular. The most Italian of all foods, pasta itself, was first created on this beautiful island during the time of the Arab domination. The oldest known word for pasta is *maccarunne* from the Sicilian word *maccare*, meaning 'to crush', here referring to the crushing of the grain, in order to make the dough.

During the advanced civilization of Magna Graecia, which flourished in Sicily around 400 BC, the art of cooking was very highly regarded. The cook Trimalcion was a native of Syracuse and lived in the town of Gela. He became so famous for his ability and artistic invention that he was soon in demand all over the Greek world. The cook Mitecus, also of Syracuse, wrote a treatise entitled *The Sicilian Cook*, which was two thousand years ahead of its time. A cook called Laoduco, around the same time, opened the first paying school for hotel management in Sicily. Cooking as an art was born in Sicily, and so it has remained throughout the island's long and complex history.

What should not be overlooked are the number of influences which Sicilian cooking has undergone: Greek, Roman, Norman, Angevin, Aragonese, Spanish and even English. People from all over the western world have converged on the lovely island for centuries, usually with possession and conquest in mind, but also bringing ingredients and customs with them which have grafted themselves on to the local traditions with amazing ease.

The fundamental ingredients of Sicilian cuisine are identical to those of the rest of southern Italy: olive oil, pasta, fish, fruit, vegetables, pulses and herbs. To this intensely colourful and deliciously fragrant base, however, Sicily has added echoes and flavours from the various parts of the world which are a part of her history. They combine to make up dishes that, to anybody not familiar with the luscious cuisine of the island, can sometimes taste quite unusual.

The range of dishes is so very extensive that it is all too easy just to skim the surface. Even visiting the island, one can risk missing the very best Sicilian cuisine. The local *trattorie*, restaurants and hotels are making some effort to revive the old recipes, but real, traditional Sicilian cooking, in all its magnificence and with all its rich secrets, lives on chiefly in the privacy of Sicilian households, from the most aristocratic to the most humble.

If one traces Sicily's difficult, complicated past and the various periods of domination, one can easily trace each thread of the fabric which goes to make up the colourful tapestry of the island's culinary heritage. Magna Graecia gave Sicily olives and olive oil, salted ricotta cheese, honey, fish, lamb and wine. From the Roman period came dishes such as stuffed squid, baked onions and pulse dishes like 'maccu', a purée of beans boiled in water and herbs, flavoured with olive oil and served with bread or pasta. Although this dish is fairly rare, and you will seldom find it on a restaurant menu, it is still eaten in some of the tiny villages of inland Sicily. For centuries, it was the staple diet of peasants and sulphur miners, who would carry it to work with them in an earthenware container called a *quartara*. Sicily was at its most prosperous during the Arab domination. The island became a perfumed, luxuriant garden, growing all kinds of newly imported crops: rice, citrus fruits, sugar cane, anise, palm trees, cotton and many others. This period also brought the island other riches such as a vast range of spices for flavouring the dishes, medicinal drugs which helped to raise standards of health, and new inventions such as the complicated nets used for catching tuna fish – which are still in use today, albeit on a much smaller scale. It was also during this period that many dishes which have since come to be considered classics of Sicilian cooking were introduced: 'cuscusu' (cous cous), now the most typical speciality of the city of Taranto; 'cassata' – the most traditional, rich and sumptuous of all the famous desserts that Sicily can claim; nougat made with honey, sesame seeds and almonds; and the icy nectar made from the snow gathered on the peak of Mount Etna and flavoured with fruit juice, which the Arabs called 'sciarbat' and which led to the development of sorbet and thereafter ice cream. There is no question that Sicilian cuisine became considerably more elaborate and refined under the sophisticated rule of the Arabs.

The Angevins brought Sicily the dish known as 'farsumagru', also called 'rollò', from the French *roule*. It is still the undisputed king of the Sicilian meat dishes and is particularly significant because there are very few meat dishes among the specialities of the island. It consists of a veal roll stuffed with everything you can possibly imagine and is extraordinarily filling and luxurious. It is typical of the slightly quirky sense of humour of these islanders that the literal translation of the dish is 'false lean' – it is anything *but* lean! Another dish which has a distinctively French ancestry is 'ancidda brudacchiata', eels cooked in a wine broth with pepper, ginger, cinnamon, cloves and saffron.

After this came the period of Spanish domination under the Viceroys. When the Spanish conquistadores returned from the Americas, they brought the tomato, which was soon in use as an ingredient throughout Europe. In Southern Italy and in Sicily, the climatic conditions allowed it to flourish, and it was used in thousands of different recipes. Soon after, another vegetable from South America was introduced which has since become almost symbolic of the cuisine of Sicily: the humble eggplant, or aubergine, is a cooking ingredient which is extraordinarily close to the hearts of all Sicilian gourmets and cooks. The combination of tomatoes and aubergines in various dishes and with other ingredients, is exceptionally popular. Also from Spain came 'Pan di Spagna', a kind of plain sponge cake which literally translates as bread of Spain and which is the basis for countless Sicilian desserts; and chocolate, which is used very extensively mainly in sweet dishes but also in some savoury dishes.

The most celebrated age of Sicilian cookery is the Baronial period, when Sicily was ruled from a distance by the Aragonese, Spanish and Bourbons in turn, with the barons of these nationalities taking up residence there in order to have more direct control. Within the sumptuous residences of the ruling classes during the seventeenth and eighteenth centuries, Sicilian cuisine reached dizzy heights of opulence and magnificence. While the peasants and working-class people were practically starving, the *gattopardi* (the name given to those noblemen living in the lap of luxury), prelates and barons fought viciously over the most able *monzu* (from the French word *monsieur*, which meant master chef) who were employed specifically to create spectacular culinary inventions for their dining pleasure, and in order to impress their rivals.

What follows is a description written by Patrick Brydone, a Scottish traveller and writer, author of *Tour Through Sicily and Malta* (1773), of a luncheon given in honour of the Bishop of Agrigento in June 1770: 'There were exactly 30 of us at the table, but upon my word, I do not think there were less than a hundred dishes. They were all served with the most succulent and delicate sauces.' Having described how impressed he was with the moray eel and the livers from force-fed chickens, the author then goes on to recall one of the desserts: 'One of the waiters offered the captain a copy of a beautiful peach and, not being prepared for any trick, he didn't think it was anything else. He cut it in half, and ate a large bite. But then, with tears in his eyes, he rolled it from one side of his mouth to the other, for its great cold, and in the end he had to spit it out, saying, "My gracious, a painted snowball!"'

The great Sicilian art of making desserts, ice cream in particular, has always been a part of life on the island and has never been lost. A visit to an ice cream parlour in Messina, Palermo or Ragusa will show you what I mean. You will find an unbelievable display of *spumoni, spongati, granite, geli, pezzi duri* and *sorbetti*, in every conceivable flavour and colour, including prickly pear (which is incidentally the fruit symbol of the island), and the incredible jasmine-flavoured ices which make you want to bury your nose in their delicious scent.

The art of representation is also a very important aspect of Sicilian pastry making. Most famous is the malleable almond dough called 'pasta Reale' (Royal dough) or 'pasta della Martorana' after the famous convent where the nuns first made the dough and used it to make sweetmeats. The 'pasta' is moulded by expert craftsmen into all kinds of shapes, most specifically fruits, and then coloured. The finished pastries are not only delicious, but look just like perfect still lives.

The tradition of pastry making within the quiet walls of the local convents is one which goes back many centuries. Although it is now rare to discover the sisters at work within their convents, there are still many such institutions dotted around the island which sell delicious pastries made to secret recipes. They are made principally with ingredients that are typical of Sicilian cookery: marzipan, pistachio nuts, Sicilian candied lime, honey, almonds and ricotta cheese, and have names like *cannoli, mostaccioli, conchiglie* and the extraordinary *minni di vergine* (virgin's breasts).

The most fantastic street market in the whole of Italy has to be the amazing Vucciria in Palermo. Here you can experience a direct and very sensual contact with the essence of Sicilian cuisine. The many wares are displayed with a fantastic sense of style and colour. Among the vegetable stands there are mountains of brilliantly coloured, juicy peppers, which alternate with shiny aubergines which range in colour from white tinged with blue to a deep, intense violet. There is an incredible variety of broccoli, zucchini, marrows, salads and artichokes. The variety of fresh and dried fruit is breathtaking, and the fish stalls carry whole swordfish, red fleshed tuna and silvery sardines as well as the almost transparent, newly hatched sardines and anchovies called *nunnata*.

With all this abundance of fantastic produce, a stupendous range of dishes are created, using scent and colour as essential ingredients, and adding generous amounts of exuberance, imagination, abundance and a strong flair for decoration. In Sicilian cooking, even the most simple of pasta dishes becomes a work of art. Pasta with sardines, for example, consists of thick pasta in a sardine sauce boldly flavoured with saffron, wild fennel, sultanas and pine kernels. The effect is mind blowing, both visually and on the taste buds.

In the infinite array of other specialities, one ought to mention the presence of rice, which is best represented by the 'arancini', or fried rice balls, which are sold all over the island. The name means little oranges, as they are supposed to look like small citrus fruits. These are a perfect synthesis of many foreign influences on Sicilian cuisine: Arab for the rice and saffron, French for the sauce, Spanish for the tomato, and Greek for the fresh 'canestrato' cheese which is traditionally used to fill

the centre of the golden oranges.

Sicily was once the granary of Ancient Rome, and to this day the various cereals and pulses grown here play a vital part in the island's cookery. The main examples are wheat, barley, oats, rice, chick-peas, beans of many varieties and lentils.

Citrus fruits are synonymous with Sicily, and there is a splendid range of lemons, oranges, mandarins and clementines.

Meat is extremely rare, particularly beef, which is usually cooked as mince because of its poor quality; although there is a fairly extensive range of cured meats and sausages made from the local pork. The island has an ancient tradition of preserving vegetables in olive oil: sun dried tomatoes, olives, aubergines, peppers, onions and many others are eaten and enjoyed all over Italy as well as on the island itself.

Finally, no discussion of Sicilian food would be complete without mentioning fish. The three seas that surround the island offer fish of excellent quality, and there are countless specialities that make the most of it. 'Sarde a beccafico' a triumphant sweet-and-sour fish dish, is made differently in Palermo, Messina and Catania. In Messina, the range of recipes using swordfish is enormous and extraordinarily imaginative, and Trapani is famous for its fantastic tuna fish. The fishing fleet of Mazzaro del Valle was the first in Italy, and the tradition which spread from this harbour is still exceptionally strong all around the triangular coast of the island.

Pasta 'Ncasciata

Baked Pasta Mould

The word *'ncasciata* actually means shut up in a box, although the same word can be used to mean containing lots of cheese, as in the local Ragusa dialect, so there is often much confusion over which dish is actually being referred to! The cheese used is caciocavallo, although fresh mozzarella can be substituted. Like the architecture of the city that this dish comes from, it has a decidedly decadent, baroque air about it.

Serves 6

4 aubergines (eggplants), cut into
    2cm/¾in thick slices
salt and freshly milled black pepper
600ml/1 pint/2½ cups olive oil
2 cloves garlic, peeled and lightly crushed
6 fresh basil leaves, whole
1kg/2lb fresh tomatoes, peeled, seeded and
    quartered
125g/4oz veal escalope (scallop), cubed
125g/4oz chicken livers, trimmed and
    chopped
125g/4oz/1 cup frozen or fresh peas,
    cooked
500g/1lb maccheroni
125g/4oz caciocavallo or mozzarella
    cheese, very thinly sliced
3 slices salame Milano, chopped
9 leaves fresh basil, torn into shreds
3 hard-boiled eggs, sliced
75g/3oz/¾ cup freshly grated pecorino
    cheese
extra 2 tablespoons olive oil for greasing

Lay the aubergine (eggplant) slices in a colander and scatter generously with salt. Cover with a plate, put a weight on top of the plate, put the colander in the sink and leave to drain for about 30 minutes. Remove the aubergines from the colander, rinse and pat them dry.

Heat 500ml/¾ pint/2 cups olive oil until sizzling hot and fry the aubergine slices on both sides for about 3 minutes. Drain well on kitchen paper (paper towels) and set aside. Throw away the oil used for frying.

Pour the remaining fresh olive oil into a saucepan and gently fry the garlic and basil leaves until the garlic is dark brown. Remove the garlic and stir in the tomatoes. Season and add the veal, chicken livers and peas. Simmer slowly for about 45 minutes.

Preheat the oven to 180°C/450°F/Gas Mark 4. When the sauce is ready, bring a large pan of salted water to a rolling boil. Toss in the pasta, stir, return to the boil and cook until just tender. Drain well and transfer it to a large bowl. Add half the sauce, the caciocavallo, salame and hard-boiled eggs to the pasta and mix everything together very carefully. Use almost all the fried aubergine slices to line a greased 850ml/1½ pint/3¾ cup smooth sided mould. Chop the remaining aubergine slices finely and stir them into the sauce.

Pour the dressed pasta into the lined mould and pat down the top with the back of a spoon. Cover the top with the pecorino and bang the mould down firmly on the tabletop to settle all the ingredients. Bake for about 20 minutes, then leave to rest for 5 minutes. Turn out on to a warmed serving platter to serve with the remaining piping hot sauce offered separately.

Pasta con la Mollica

Pasta with Breadcrumbs

The recipe here is the western version of this very
typical dish prepared all over Southern Italy.

Serves 4

salt
75ml/3fl oz/6 tablespoons olive oil
2 large cloves garlic, lightly crushed
125g/4oz salted anchovies, rinsed, dried
   and boned
3 tablespoons chopped fresh parsley
500g/1lb/2½ cups fresh tomatoes, peeled,
   quartered and seeded
salt and freshly milled black pepper
350g/12oz penne, maccheroni, bucatini or
   similar shaped dried durum
wheat pasta
75g/3oz stale white bread

Bring a large pan of salted water to a rolling boil
for the pasta. Preheat the oven to 230°C/
450°F/Gas Mark 8. In a separate saucepan, heat
half the oil with garlic until the garlic is brown.
Discard the garlic and add the anchovies. Mash
thoroughly into the oil, then stir in the parsley and
the tomatoes and season.

   Crush the bread into coarse crumbs, then mix
with the remaining oil and scatter them all over a
baking sheet. Brown in the oven for about 5
minutes, taking care that they do not burn.

   Toss the pasta into the boiling water, stir, return
to the boil and cook until the pasta is just tender.
Drain well and return it to the pan. Pour over the
sauce and toss it all together. Transfer into an
ovenproof serving dish and scatter with the toasted
breadcrumbs. Return to the oven for 2 minutes
before serving.

Sfinciuni

Simple Onion and Tomato Pizza

There is always discussion as to the origins of this
speciality, and friends of mine have been driven to
using quite strong language in their defence of the
dish as having Campanian origins. I am convinced
that it is Sicilian, that it has ancient roots and that
it is sometimes called *schiavazza* or *sciaguazza*. Indeed,
one of the most famous *sfinciuni* ever made was
prepared by the nuns of the San Vito and there is
still a famous *Sfinciuni di Santu Vitu* enjoyed in the
city of Palermo.

   Sometimes, large quantities of fresh sausage are
added to the topping, which actually becomes a
filling as a second layer of dough is rolled out and
used to cover the pizza completely.

Makes one 17.5cm/7in pizza, 10cm/4in deep

250g/8oz/2 cups plain white (all-
   purpose) flour
salt and freshly milled black pepper
12 tablespoons freshly grated pecorino or
   caciocavallo cheese
250ml/8fl oz/1 cup olive oil
juice of 1 lemon
15g/½oz fresh yeast
500g/1lb fresh ripe tomatoes
50g/2oz/1 cup fresh parsley, finely
   chopped
5 large salted anchovies, rinsed, dried,
   boned and chopped
1 small onion, finely sliced
1 heaped tablespoon fresh coarse white
   breadcrumbs
extra 3–4 tablespoons plain white flour for
   dusting and kneading

Pile all the flour on the tabletop and make a hollow in the centre with your fist. Add ½ teaspoon each of salt and pepper and 4 tablespoons of grated cheese. Heat 3 tablespoons of the olive oil with the lemon juice until hand hot, then pour this into the hollow. Crumble the yeast into 5 tablespoons of hand-hot water, stir thoroughly and pour this into the hollow also. Knead everything together, adding as much warm water as you need to make a smooth, elastic dough. Knead thoroughly and energetically for a further 10–15 minutes. Roll the dough into a ball and place it in a large bowl. Cut a cross shape across the top of the ball and cover it with a cloth, then leave it to rise for 2 hours in a warm place, until doubled in size.

Meanwhile, dip the tomatoes into boiling hot water and peel them. Cut them all in half, remove the seeds and chop them coarsely. Pour 4 tablespoons of the olive into a saucepan and fry the onion until soft and transparent. Add the tomatoes, season with salt and pepper and simmer very slowly for 1 hour. Meanwhile, grease a 17.5cm/7in deep springform or loose-bottom cake tin (pan) very thoroughly, or line with greased baking parchment, if you prefer.

Take the risen dough out of the bowl, knock it back and knead for about 10 minutes. Place in the cake pan and leave to rise again in a warm place for about 30 minutes.

Meanwhile, add the parsley, half the anchovies and half the remaining grated cheese to the tomato sauce, mixing all together. Preheat the oven to 200°C/400°F/Gas Mark 6. When the dough has risen again, bury your fingers deep into the dough at even distances to make several little hollows. Fill the hollows with tomato sauce, and spread a little more sauce all over the surface, reserving a little sauce back for later use. Bake the *sfinciuni* for 25 minutes, until golden brown around the edges.

Heat about 3 tablespoons of the remaining oil in a small frying pan (skillet) and fry the breadcrumbs until brown and crisp. Take the pizza out of the oven and add the remaining tomato sauce, the rest of the anchovies and cheese and then scatter the fried breadcrumbs over the whole thing. Finish off with a dousing of olive oil and return to the oven to bake for a further 10 minutes. Remove from the oven and serve at once.

Pasta con le Sarde

Pasta with Fresh Sardines

What gives the dish its almost unique flavour is the use of wild fennel which is boiled, and then the same water is used to cook the pasta. I really like the combination of flavours provided by the saffron, the fresh fish and the aniseed taste of the fennel. Of course, if you cannot get hold of fresh sardines, you can use frozen. If wild fennel proves difficult to find in your local hedgerows or fields, buy some relatively leafy fennel bulbs and trim off all the feathery leaves, then use the hard outer leaves and the stalks (stems) to make up the weight.

Serves 4

150g/5oz wild fennel (leaves and stalks), rinsed and carefully trimmed
2 teaspoons fine salt
1 large onion, peeled and chopped
6-7 tablespoons olive oil
1 sachet saffron powder, about 125mg
30g/1¼oz/¼ cup pine kernels
30g/1¼oz sultanas (golden raisins), soaked in warm water for 15 minutes, then drained
300g/10oz sardines, defrosted if frozen, gutted, boned and headless
2 salted anchovies, rinsed, dried and boned
salt and freshly milled black pepper
400g/14oz bucatini or thick perciatelli

Pasta con le Sarde/Pasta with Fresh Sardines

Put the fennel in a large saucepan of salted water. Bring to the boil, then cover and simmer for about 10 minutes. Remove the fennel, drain well and squeeze dry, reserving all the water as it will be used to cook the pasta. Chop the fennel finely.

Put the onion in a large saucepan and cover generously with water. Simmer until the onion is soft, then add about 3½ tablespoons olive oil, the saffron diluted in 3 tablespoons cold water, the pine kernels and the sultanas (golden raisins). Simmer together, stirring frequently, for about 10 minutes. Stir in the fennel. Add the sardines, cover the saucepan and simmer very slowly, turning the fish over frequently.

In a separate pan, fry the anchovies in the remaining olive oil, mashing them into a smooth brown purée. When the sardines are cooked through, add the anchovy purée to the sardines. Mix it all together and season to taste with salt and pepper. Keep warm until the pasta is cooked.

Bring a large pan containing the salted fennel water to a rolling boil. Toss in the pasta and stir, return to the boil and cook until just tender. Drain well, transfer to a warmed bowl, pour over the sauce and toss thoroughly. Serve at once.

Caponata di Pesce

Lobster Caponata

The first time I prepared this really rather bizarre dish was on the radio for *Woman's Hour* on BBC Radio 4. A listener had apparently been served the dish on holiday and was anxious to know how to make it. I have since had occasion to wonder whether it was, in fact, this version of the ubiquitous Caponata which the gourmet listener had enjoyed, but having discovered how weird and wonderful this one actually is, it was hard to go back to any of the other versions. Trust the

Sicilians to go for a Caponata which is completely over the top compared to any of the other versions! It does taste delicious, well worth trying it out!

Serves 8

4 aubergines (eggplants), cut into strips
salt and freshly milled black pepper
4 tablespoons white wine vinegar
1 carrot, scraped and quartered
1 onion, peeled and quartered
1 stick celery
1 sprig fresh thyme
3 sprigs fresh parsley
2 bay leaves
1 small, live lobster, weighing about 800g/1¾lb
1.8 litre/3 pints/7½ cups sunflower oil
4 heads celery, all hard exterior stalks (stems) removed
300g/10 pickling (pearl) onions, peeled
4 tablespoons olive oil
2 tablespoons caster (superfine) sugar
3 tablespoons red wine vinegar
500g/1lb/2½ cups ripe tomatoes, peeled, quartered and seeded
1 clove garlic, chopped
2 tablespoons chopped fresh parsley
1 tablespoon salted capers, well rinsed and dried
200g/7oz/1⅓ cups stoned black (pitted ripe) olives
300g/10oz octopus or squid, cut into strips and ready to cook
5 tablespoons plain white (all-purpose) flour

for the sauce:

125g/4oz/1 cup flaked (slivered) almonds

2 tablespoons olive oil

50g/2oz stale white bread

3 salted anchovies, rinsed, dried and boned

juice of 1 orange

25g/1oz/¼ cup icing (confectioners')
    sugar, sifted

25g/1oz/¼ cup finely grated chocolate

3 tablespoons red wine vinegar

to garnish:

4 hard-boiled eggs, sliced into segments

300g/10oz cooked unshelled prawns
    (shrimps)

Put the aubergines in a colander and cover with salt. Put a plate on top and a weight on top of the plate. Put the colander in the sink and leave it to drain out the bitter juices from the aubergines for about 2 hours.

Meanwhile, fill a fish kettle or large saucepan with water and add the vinegar, carrot, onion, celery stick, the herbs and about 1 teaspoon salt. Bring to the boil, then simmer, covered, for about 10 minutes. Return to the boil and slide in the lobster, head first. Allow the lobster to simmer for 15 minutes, then take it off the heat and leave it to cool in the liquid.

Rinse and pat dry the aubergines. Cut the strips into cubes. Strip the celery heads to the hearts, then cut each heart into strips from the top to the bottom, being sure not to cut them completely. You should end up with large flowers or stars.

Pour half the sunflower seed oil into a deep-fat fryer and heat until a small piece of bread dropped into it sizzles instantly. Fry the aubergine cubes and the celery hearts until golden and softened. Drain well on kitchen paper (paper towels) and discard the oil.

Pour about 1 litre/1¾ pints/4½ cups cold water into a saucepan and bring to the boil. Drop in the onions and simmer for 10 minutes, then drain well.

In a separate saucepan, fry the onions in about 4 tablespoons of the olive oil until slightly browned, then sprinkle with the sugar. Gently fry for a further 5 minutes, stirring frequently, then stir in the vinegar. Boil off the alcohol and leave the vinegar to reduce by half, then add the tomatoes. Mix together, season and cover. Leave to simmer for about 30 minutes, adding water occasionally if the onions appear to be drying out too much.

Mix the garlic and parsley together. Heat the remaining sunflower oil until a small piece of bread dropped into it sizzles instantly. Toss the octopus or squid in the flour, then fry in oil until crisp. Drain well on kitchen paper (paper towels).

Add the garlic and parsley, capers and olives to the onion and tomato mixture. Season with salt and pepper, then mix in the fried aubergines and celery. Continue simmering slowly.

Take the lobster out of its cooking liquid and cut it open. Remove all the flesh. Set the claws aside and slice the remaining flesh into small pieces. Add this to the other ingredients. Finally mixed in the fried octopus or squid strips and heat everything through.

Cook for a further 5–10 minutes so that the flavours have a chance to amalgamate, then turn it all out on to a platter and leave it to cool down. While it cools make the sauce.

Fry the almonds and oil in a small pan until the almonds are well browned. Tip this mixture into the food processor and add the stale bread. Whizz until mixed together, then add the anchovies and the orange juice. Whizz again. Turn this mixture into a small saucepan and add the sugar and chocolate and the vinegar and 3 tablespoons cold water. Stir this mixture over a medium heat for about 5 minutes, then take it off the heat and strain it through a fine sieve (strainer).

When the main ingredients have cooled sufficiently, shape them into a mound and cover completely with the sauce. Garnish with the hard-boiled eggs and prawns (shrimps). Arrange the lobster claws on top and serve.

Vermicelli al Nero di Seppie

Vermicelli with Squid Ink

Like so many of the pasta dishes from this island, this recipe is amazingly rich and filling, mainly because in harder times not so long ago, the pasta course would have represented the entire meal. This simple rule of parsimony has since evolved into an eating tradition. This recipe is typical of the small towns and villages which sit at the feet of Mount Etna, although quite often the locals prefer to substitute rice for the pasta. With rice, the dish takes on the flavour and texture of the Venetian dish of *risotto nero* and somehow looses something of its intrinsic Sicilian style.

For real authenticity, the recipe needs a good dose of *strattu*, the inimitable dried tomato concentrate which is made by simply drying out tomatoes in the baking hot sun and then pounding them into a purée and maturing the result in yet more sunlight. If you cannot get hold of this almost unexported speciality, use ordinary concentrated tomato purée (paste), commonly sold in cans, jars or tubes.

Serves 4

500g/1lb whole squid, including ink sac
4 tablespoons olive oil
2–3 cloves garlic, lightly crushed
3 tablespoons chopped fresh parsley
salt and freshly milled black pepper
125ml/4fl oz/½ cup dry white wine
1 tablespoon *strattu*, or 3 tablespoons
    concentrated tomato purée (paste)
400g/14oz vermicelli

Clean the squid by removing the beaks, eyes and inner bones. Carefully remove the ink sacs and set them aside. Peel the outer film of skin from the bodies of the squid, then cut the bodies into small cubes. Chop all the tentacles finely. Rinse and dry all the fish very thoroughly.

Heat the olive oil in large saucepan and fry the garlic until brown, then discard. Add the squid, parsley and plenty of pepper. Stir together and simmer, covered, for about 45 minutes.

Pour over the white wine and stir in the tomato purée (paste) and simmer, uncovered, for about 20 minutes. Lower the heat further, cover and continue simmering for a further 30 minutes, occasionally adding a little hot water to dilute the sauce.

Half an hour before you want to eat, bring a large pan of salted water to a rolling boil. Toss in the pasta, stir, return to the boil and cook until just tender. Drain well and return to the pan.

When the pasta is put into the boiling water, add the ink sacs to the sauce and stir it all together. Pour the sauce over the cooked pasta and mix together very thoroughly. Cover and leave to stand for about 5 minutes, then turn out on to a warmed serving platter. Serve at once.

Triglie col Finocchio
Red Mullet with Fennel

It is quite unusual to find fish cooked with lard in this way, although the familiar Sicilian flavours of aniseed and lemon would tell you where this dish came from even if you were made to taste it blindfolded.

Serves 4

8 small red mullet, gutted and scaled, rinsed and patted dry
125ml/4fl oz/½ cup olive oil
juice of 1 lemon
salt and freshly milled black pepper
1 heaped teaspoon fennel seeds
125g/4oz/½ cup lard
2 tablespoons chopped fresh parsley
1 lemon, sliced into wedges

Arrange the fish in a deep dish and cover them with the oil, making sure it also goes inside each fish. Pour over the lemon juice and season generously, inside and out, with salt and plenty of freshly milled black pepper. Crush the fennel seeds to a powder and mix with the lard. Smear this mixture inside and outside each fish. Preheat the grill (broiler) to a medium level.

Wrap each fish in foil and place under a medium grill to cook on both sides for 15–20 minutes altogether, or until the foil is puffed out and the fish smells cooked. You can check by opening one package and piercing the fish with a sharp knife to make sure the flesh is flaky and cooked right through.

Unwrap and arrange on a platter with the lemon wedges. Serve at once.

Baccalà al Pomodoro
Dried Salt Cod with Tomato Sauce

This is a very traditional and typical Sicilian recipe, although why they should want to use *baccalà* with such a passion when they have a whole sea full of fresh fish available to them is quite beyond me. I suppose I just concede that salt cod (cooked properly) is a good standby when fresh fish is less plentiful at certain times during the year.

This recipe has lots of different versions. In some households, for example, the fish is deep-fried and then covered in sauce, while in others, sultanas (golden raisins) and pine kernels are liberally added to the sauce. In still other households the fish is baked instead of fried. Wherever you might eat this, however, it is quite common for the dish to be served either as an antipasto or as a main course.

Serves 4

800g/1¾lb dried salt cod, soaked for 3 days in fresh cold water, changed regularly
75ml/3fl oz/5 tablespoons olive oil
500g/1lb/2½ cups fresh ripe tomatoes, peeled, quartered and seeded
½ teaspoon sugar
2 dry bay leaves
50g/2oz/⅓ cup stoned black (pitted ripe) olives, coarsely chopped
½ teaspoon dried thyme
salt and freshly milled black pepper

When the fish is soft, remove all traces of skin and all bones. Cut it into even-sized, large chunks.

Heat the oil until sizzling hot, then lay the fish in the oil and seal it on each side. Add the tomatoes, sugar, bay leaves and olives. Mix gently and sprinkle with the thyme and salt and pepper.

Cover and simmer very gently for 45 minutes, until the fish flakes easily. Serve at once or cool completely and serve lightly chilled.

Cuscusu di Trapani

Fish Couscous

This is another Arab speciality which the Sicilians fell in love with so many centuries ago, and which is still extremely popular all over the island, particularly on the western side and on the outlying islets. It is so popular, in fact, that locally they have created tiny pasta shapes of the same name which are used to put into soups and should not be confused with the semolina used for this dish. I am giving you a much simplified version of this age-old recipe. This is a recipe from the city of Trapani.

Serves 8

for the couscous:
1–3 sachets powdered saffron, each
   weighing 25g/1oz
400g/14oz couscous
¼ teasoon ground cinnamon
⅛ teaspoon grated nutmeg
6 tablespoons olive oil
salt and freshly milled black pepper

for the fish stew:
6 tablespoons olive oil
3 cloves garlic, chopped
4 tablespoons chopped fresh parsley
1 onion, peeled and finely sliced
1 dried bay leaf
1 tomato, peeled, quartered and seeded
1.7kg/3½lb assorted fish, such as cod, eel,
   red mullet, John Dory
salt and freshly milled black pepper

Mix the saffron powder with 125ml/4fl oz/½ cup hot water. Stir into the couscous. Spread the couscous out on to a cloth to dry out and begin to make the fish stew.

Set aside on the cloth to drain and begin to cook the fish stew. Put 6 tablespoons olive oil in a very wide, deep pan with the garlic and parsley. Fry together gently for about 5 minutes, then add the onion and the bay leaf. Fry for a further 5 minutes, then add the tomato. Stir together, then lay the fish on top of the other ingredients, preferably in a single layer. Season with salt and pepper and cover with approximately 2 litres/3½ pints/9 cups cold water. Cover and simmer slowly for about 20 minutes, until the fish flakes easily.

When the fish is all cooked, take the fish out with a slotted spoon and remove all the skin and bones. Set aside the fish and strain the fish stock carefully. Put about 500ml/¾ pint/2 cups to one side and keep it hot by putting it in a bowl placed over a pan of simmering water. Pour the remaining stock into a separate saucepan and add as much water as is necessary to make a full 2 litres/3½ pints/9 cups liquid.

Arrange a large colander or sieve (strainer) over the saucepan containing the large amount of stock and wrap the gap around the edges with a wet bandage to avoid any steam whatsoever from escaping during the cooking process. This is very important. Line the colander with very fine muslin.

Pour the couscous into the colander or sieve.

Stir the olive oil into the couscous and cover the colander or sieve with a lid. Cover the lid with a very heavy, thick cloth. Place over a low heat and steam the couscous for about 1½ hours, until tender.

Tip the cooked couscous into a bowl and add a little of the reserved fish stock. Cover with a lid and then wrap the bowl and the lid in a heavy, woollen cloth. Place this bundle in a very low oven Gas Mark ½ or the airing cupboard or over the boiler to stand for about 1 hour, occasionally stirring in a little more of the hot reserved stock. The couscous should gradually become more and more fluffy and swollen.

Re-heat the fish over a pan of simmering water. Season the couscous with the spices and arrange it all in a big mound on a platter. Sprinkle the couscous with the rest of the reserved fish stock and then arrange the fish on top. Serve at once.

Vastedde di Ragusa

Pentecost Bread

Guastedde or *vastedde* is a kind of sandwich which is prepared all over the Palermo province. If the filling ingredients of beef spleen and cheese are a little on the lean side, the loaf is called *schetta*, which means spinsterish. Only when there are plenty of tasty extra ingredients in the bread alongside the beef spleen and cheese can it be called *maritata*, which means married. Obviously, in Sicily at least, it is certainly considered preferable to be married!

In Ragusa, the bread is prepared around Pentecost time in single large loaves with elderflowers kneaded into the dough. Eating these sandwiches is supposed to be very lucky, so vast quantities of them are sold from kiosks and specialist bakers all over the city. I will give you the Ragusa version, as we could all do with a little bit of extra luck! The sandwiches, which are very much a part of the street food scene which exists in Palermo and other large cities, are also called *panu cu' la meuza*.

500g/1lb/3¾ cups strong white (bread) flour
125g/4oz plain white bread dough
125g/4oz fresh elderflowers
25g/1oz/2 tablespoons plain white (all-purpose) flour
3 tablespoons sesame seeds
225g/8oz beef spleen, trimmed and sliced into thin strips
150g/5oz/⅔ cup lard
salt and freshly milled black pepper
225g/8oz/1 cup ricotta cheese, cut into slivers
225g/8oz caciocavallo or pecorino cheese, cut into thin slices
extra lard for greasing baking sheet

Knead the flour and the bread dough together very thoroughly. Sprinkle in the elderflowers and use both hands to knead. Add enough warm water to make a smooth and elastic dough. Put aside to rise in a warm place to double in volume. Meanwhile, grease a large baking sheet with lard and sprinkle it with flour.

Cuscusu di Trapani/Fish Couscous (page 177)

Knock back the dough and shape the loaf to look like a large wheel – make a circle and then cut deep criss-cross grooves across the wheel from one side to the other to form the 'spokes'. Arrange on the greased and floured baking tray, then rub the surface of the loaf all over with cold water. Scatter sesame seeds all over the top of the loaf and leave it to rise for another hour, until doubled in size.

Meanwhile, fry the spleen gently in half the lard until cooked through, then sprinkle generously with salt and freshly milled black pepper. Melt down the remaining lard and keep it in a saucepan so you can heat it to sizzling hot when the bread is baked and the sandwiches are ready to be assembled. Preheat the oven to 190°C/375°F/Gas Mark 5. Bake the loaf for 20 minutes, until golden brown and crisp and it sounds hollow when tapped on the bottom. Divide it all into wedges following the lines of the spokes while still hot. Split open the hot bread and fill with a slice of ricotta, a little spleen and a slice of strong cheese like caciovallo or pecorino. Drizzle over some sizzling hot lard and press the sandwich closed. Eat immediately.

Sarde a Beccafico

Baked Stuffed Fresh Sardines

The name *beccafico* refers to the bird called a warbler in English, although I much prefer the literal translation from the Italian, which means pecker of figs! Obviously, somebody must have noted that these little birds like to hang themselves from the ripe fruit and peck away at the sweet flesh and

seeds to their hearts content! By stuffing the sardines practically to bursting point, and arranging their rounded bellies, and by raising their tails in a certain way to represent the open beak, with an awful lot of imagination one could imagine that the fish resemble the birds enough to be named after them . . . although I think there is a certain amount of cook's fantasy mixed up in the name of this dish, which gives it a charm of its own.

I am giving you the recipe from the eastern side of the island, because I think it is far more interesting and exotic than the recipe from the western side, in which the fish have a much simpler filling and are then coated in breadcrumbs and fried instead of being baked. Both recipes, however, are absolutely delicious, especially if the sardines are completely fresh.

Serves 4

125ml/4fl oz/½ cup olive oil
750g/1½lb sardines, defrosted if frozen
3 heaped tablespoons fresh white
    breadcrumbs
50g/2oz/¼ cup sultanas (golden raisins),
    soaked in warm water for 15 minutes
    and drained
50g/2oz/⅓ cup pine kernels
2 tablespoons chopped fresh parsley
salt and freshly milled black pepper
6 salted anchovies, rinsed, dried, boned and
    finely chopped
3–4 dried bay leaves

Pre-heat the oven to 180°C/350°F/Gas Mark 4. Grease an ovenproof serving dish with half the oil. Slit open the fish and remove the innards with your fingers, holding the fish under running water. Holding the fish flat on its back on the worktop, with its tail pointing towards you. Pull the head down towards you, removing the spine and all the bones along with the head, but leaving on the tail and keeping the fish intact. This is a lot easier to do than it sounds!

Slowly heat the remaining oil in a saucepan with 1 tablespoon of the breadcrumbs. Stir together to amalgamate them carefully, then take off the heat. Drain and dry the sultanas (golden raisins). Stir them into the breadcrumb and oil mixture, then add the pine kernels and the parsley. Season with salt and pepper, then stir the anchovies into the mixture.

Insert stuffing into each of the fish to make them plump and rounded. Arrange the fish in the dish with their tails pointing upwards. Drizzle with oil and scatter over the remaining breadcrumbs. Bake for 30 minutes, until the fish flakes easily. Serve at once.

Truscello di Messina

Meatball and Ricotta Bake

This is the sort of dish which used to be traditional of the city of Messina, although sadly it has been superseded (like so many things) by the lure of fast food and 'quick 'n easy' dishes. Some families who retain their ancient traditions better than others still prepare their *truscello* on special occasions. The most vital ingredient is the fresh ricotta.

Serves 6

300g/10oz lean minced (ground) beef
salt and freshly milled black pepper
125g/4oz/1 cup freshly grated Parmesan
    cheese
125g/4oz/1 cup stale white breadcrumbs
5 eggs
3 tablespoons chopped fresh parsley
500ml/¾ pint/2 cups very strong
    flavoured beef stock
300g/10oz fresh ricotta
1¼ teaspoon ground cloves

Mix the minced (ground) beef with plenty of salt and pepper, 2 tablespoons of the Parmesan, the breadcrumbs, 2 of the eggs, parsley and a tiny amount of stock to bind it all together. Shape these into tiny meatballs no larger than big olives.

Bring the stock to the boil, then simmer the meatballs in the stock for no more than 5 minutes. Take off the heat. Preheat the oven to 200°C/400°F/Gas Mark 6.

Mix the remaining Parmesan with the ricotta, the remaining 3 eggs, salt and pepper and the ground cloves. Shape this mixture into balls the same size as the meatballs.

Pour a little stock into the bottom of an ovenproof serving dish. Cover with a layer of the ricotta balls, then cover with a layer of meatballs. Cover with more stock and continue in this way until all the ingredients have been used. Bake for about 5 minutes. Serve at once.

Melanzane, Pomodori e Peperoni Arrosto

Baked Aubergines, Tomatoes and Peppers

This is a deliciously rustic kind of salad, which is prepared all over the island. Char-grilled vegetables served with just a drizzle of olive oil and a sprinkling of chopped parsley, salt and pepper have become one of the most popular and fashionable dishes served in trendy restaurants all over the world – whether they are Italian or not. This is a variation on that theme, and a forerunner of the modern dish.

Originally the dish required a wood fire on which to barbecue the vegetables, it is also very good when prepared with a domestic grill (broiler).

Serves 4

4 aubergines (eggplants), sliced into finger thick slices
salt and freshly milled black pepper
5 large, ripe marmanade tomatoes
200ml/7fl oz/14 tablespoons olive oil
5 peppers, assorted colours, rinsed and dried
2 tablespoons chopped fresh parsley
2 cloves garlic, crushed and chopped

Coat the aubergine (eggplant) slices with salt and lay them all in a colander. Cover with a plate, place a weight on top of the plate and put the colander in the sink. Leave to drain for about 2 hours, then rinse and pat dry.

Meanwhile, lay the tomatoes under or over high heat (depending upon whether you are using a barbecue, grill or broiler) and grill them until the skins blister and crack, brushing frequently with olive oil. Remove the skins and chop all the flesh from the slightly cooked tomatoes, discarding the seeds. Put the chopped tomatoes in a salad bowl.

Grill the peppers all over, brushing with olive oil. Cut them in half and discard the seeds and membranes. Slice the peppers into thin strips and put these in the salad bowl as well.

Grill the aubergine slices, brushing with olive oil, and then cut these into thin strips and add them to the tomatoes and peppers.

Dress with the remaining olive oil, salt and pepper to taste, chopped parsley and garlic. Mix it all together and leave to stand for about 15 minutes before serving.

Zucchine in Agrodolce

Sweet-and-sour Courgettes

Probably one of the most typical dishes of the island, which brings together all the different flavours and textures which make Sicilian cooking so unique.

Serves 4

4 tablespoons olive oil
2 cloves garlic, crushed
4 large courgettes (zucchini), topped and tailed, peeled and cut into matchsticks
2 large teaspoons red wine vinegar
2 salted anchovies, rinsed, dried and boned
1 tablespoon sultanas (golden raisins), soaked in warm water for 15 minutes, then drained and dried
1 tablespoon pine kernels
¼ teaspoon sugar
salt

Melanzane, Pomodori e Peperoni Arrosto / Baked Aubergines,
Tomatoes and Peppers

Heat the oil and garlic together until the garlic is brown, then discard it. Add the courgette (zucchini) sticks and fry them for about 10 minutes or until just tender. Stir in the vinegar, anchovies, sultanas (golden raisins) and the pine kernels. Mix it all together and sprinkle with sugar. Cook for a further 10 minutes, or until the courgettes are completely soft. Season with salt only if required. Serve hot.

Riso e Melanzane alla Palermitana

Rice and Aubergine Bake

The aubergine (eggplant) has to be the vegetable most used in all the different parts of Sicily, throughout the whole meal from the antipasto to the pudding, ever since the Arabs first introduced it to the island. The use of rice in this recipe is another reflection of the strong Eastern influence which crops up in many local recipes.

Serves 6

3 aubergines (eggplants), cut into 2cm/¾in slices
salt and freshly milled black pepper
2 onions, peeled
6 tablespoons olive oil
50g/2oz/¼ cup unsalted butter
2 tablespoons chopped fresh parsley
8 leaves fresh basil, torn into shreds
300g/10oz/1½ cups fresh tomatoes, peeled, quartered and seeded
300g/10oz/1½ cups risotto rice
600ml/1 pint/2½ cups chicken or vegetable stock, kept boiling hot
3 tablespoons plain white (all-purpose) flour
about 750ml/1¼ pints/3 cups sunflower oil
125g/4oz/1 cup freshly grated caciocavallo cheese
2 tablespoons olive oil for greasing

Lay the aubergine (eggplant) slices in a colander and sprinkle them generously with salt. Cover with a plate, put a weight on top of the plate, put the colander in the sink and leave the aubergines to drain for 1–2 hours, then rinse and pat dry.

Put the onions in a saucepan and cover generously with water. Boil for 10 minutes, then drain and discard the water.

Put 3 tablespoons of the olive oil in a saucepan with the butter. Slice 1 onion finely and fry it in the oil and butter until soft. Stir in the parsley and the basil and continue frying. After about 5 minutes, add the tomatoes and season with salt and pepper. Cover and simmer slowly for about 20 minutes, stirring occasionally. Preheat the oven to Gas Mark 2.

Slice the remaining onion and fry it slowly in a flameproof casserole in the remaining oil. Add the rice once the onion is transparent. Mix until the rice is shiny, then add the stock and stir thoroughly. Put the rice into the oven for 15 minutes. Dust the aubergine slices lightly with flour.

Heat the sunflower seed oil in a large frying pan (skillet) until sizzling hot, then fry the aubergine slices for 3 minutes on both sides. Drain them well on kitchen paper (paper towels).

Take the rice out of the oven and stir in 2–3 tablespoons of grated caciocavallo. Grease a 1.2kg/2½lb smooth, round mould with the oil. Line the bottom with aubergine slices. Cover with a layer of tomato sauce, then with a layer of rice and then a generous sprinkling of grated caciocavallo.

Continue making these layers until the mould is full, banging it down firmly on the tabletop every now and again to settle the ingredients. Finish off with a sprinkling of cheese.

Place the mould in the oven to bake for about 10 minutes. Remove from the oven and turn out to serve at once.

Polpette di Funghi
Mushroom Fritters

The mushrooms traditionally used for this recipe are called *pignolini*, and they are similar to porcini in appearance. They grow at the base of conifer trees, and therefore retain a slightly resinous, pine-like flavour – hence their name. They tend to be quite soft and spongey, rather than fleshy, and are perfect for this sort of dish. Whatever mushrooms you choose, make sure they have a soft texture.

Makes 24

500g/1lb mushrooms (see above), wiped clean
2 eggs, beaten
3 cloves garlic, very finely chopped
3 tablespoons chopped fresh parsley
2 heaped tablespoons grated pecorino cheese
2 heaped tablespoons fresh white breadcrumbs
salt and freshly milled black pepper
750ml/1¼ pints/3 cups sunflower oil

Steam the cleaned mushrooms until just tender. Drain well, then chop them very finely in a food processor. Add the eggs, the garlic, parsley, cheese and breadcrumbs and season with salt and plenty of freshly milled black pepper. Mix this all together very thoroughly, then shape into 24 smallish, flat circles.

Heat the oil until a small piece of bread dropped into it sizzles instantly. Fry the fritters until crisp and golden all over, frying in batches, if necessary. Drain well on kitchen paper (paper towels). Serve at once.

Pignolata
New Year's Eve Cake

This is the traditional New Year's Eve cake of Messina, although it is much loved, eaten and prepared all over the island. Even the emigrants who crossed the ocean to go to the United States took this wonderful dessert with them to remind themselves of their homeland. When you buy the cake in the local pastry shops of Messina, it is usually prepared in two colours with some of the cake covered in chocolate. Warning, like many Sicilian desserts, this one is incredibly sweet!

500g/1lb/4 cups plain white (all-purpose) flour
7 whole eggs
5 more eggs, separated
2 tablespoons lard
25ml/1fl oz/2 tablespoons pure edible alcohol spirit
1 litre/1¾ pints/4½ cups sunflower oil
500g/1lb/2½ cups caster (superfine) sugar
grated rind (peel) of 1 lemon

Pile the flour on the worktop and make a hollow in the centre with your fist. Break the 7 whole eggs into the hollow. Add the 5 egg yolks and the lard. Knead it all together with your hands until the flour has absorbed all the eggs. Add the alcohol spirit to the dough 1 drop at a time.

Heat the oil until a small piece of bread dropped into it sizzles instantly. Roll the dough into thin cylinders, then cut it into 3cm/1¼in cubes. Drop the cubes into the hot oil and fry them until puffy, golden and crisp. Drain well on kitchen paper (paper towels).

Pour half the sugar into a saucepan and melt it over a medium heat, stirring constantly and vigorously in the same direction until it has turned to a smooth caramel. Tip all the fried pastry on to a heatproof platter and pour over the hot caramel, pulling the mixture into a mountain shape as you go along with a spatula.

Melt the remaining sugar in a saucepan until blond coloured. Beat the egg whites until completely dry and stiff, then beat in the melted sugar very quickly. Stir in the grated lemon rind (peel) and coat the mound of fried pastry and caramel with the meringue. Serve at once.

Gelato di Cocomero

Watermelon Ice Cream

It is a well known fact that it was the Sicilians who invented ice cream, having been taught how to make the original version of this universal dessert by their Arab invaders. Nowhere in the world will you taste ice cream quite like it is in Sicily, and the following recipe is no exception. Make sure you use a really sweet, ripe watermelon.

Only in Sicily will you experience the flavour of ice creams with the flavour and perfume of the fruit so intact. The use of jasmine flower water is an ingredient you may have trouble finding, in which case use orange blossom water instead.

Serves 6

500g/1lb watermelon flesh (no seeds or skin)
300g/10oz/1½ cups caster (superfine) sugar
2 tablespoons jasmine flower water, or 2 teaspoons orange blossom water
125g/4oz couverture chocolate, cubed finely
40g/1½oz/⅓ cup shelled pistachio nuts, chopped
125g/4oz/⅔ cup candied pumpkin, pear, apple or melon
1 teaspoon ground cinnamon

Push the watermelon through a sieve (strainer), then mix it thoroughly with half the sugar and the jasmine flower water.

Pour it into a metal mould and freeze until slushy, stirring every 10 minutes or so to break up the ice crystals. When it is thick and slushy, stir in the chocolate, the remaining sugar, nuts, pumpkin and cinnamon. Return to the freezer and continue to freeze until solid, stirring occasionally.

When you are ready to serve, dip the mould into hot water to loosen the edges, then turn out on to a platter and serve at once.

Index